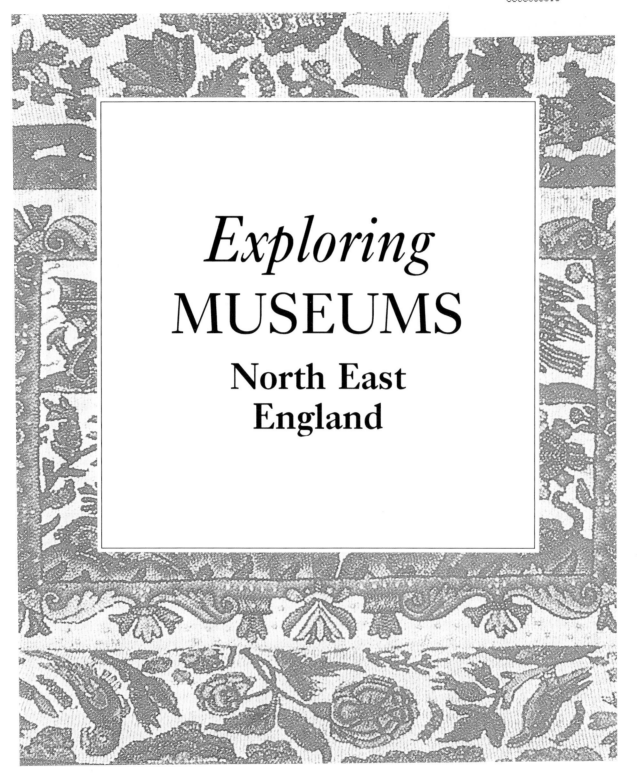

Exploring
MUSEUMS

North East
England

MUSEUMS & GALLERIES COMMISSION

A MUSEUMS ASSOCIATION GUIDE

Exploring
MUSEUMS
North East England

David Fleming

LONDON: HER MAJESTY'S STATIONERY OFFICE

© Crown Copyright 1989
First published 1989
ISBN 0 11 290470 X

British Library Cataloguing in
Publication Data
A CIP catalogue record for this book is
available from the British Library

HMSO BOOKS

HMSO publications are available from:

HMSO Publications Centre
(Mail and telephone orders only)
PO Box 276, London, SW8 5DT
Telephone orders 01–873 9090
General enquiries 01–873 0011
(queuing system in operation for both numbers)

HMSO Bookshops
49 High Holborn, London, WC1V 6HB 01–873 0011 (Counter service only)
258 Broad Street, Birmingham, B1 2HE 021–643 3740
Southey House, 33 Wine Street, Bristol, BS1 2BQ (0272) 264306
9–21 Princess Street, Manchester, M60 8AS 061–834 7201
80 Chichester Street, Belfast, BT1 4JY (0232) 238451
71 Lothian Road, Edinburgh, EH3 9AZ 031–228 4181

HMSO's Accredited Agents
(see Yellow Pages)

and through good booksellers

CONTENTS

OTHER VOLUMES IN THE SERIES

BUCKINGHAM PALACE

As Patron of Museums Year 1989, I hope that through this series of Regional Guides "Exploring Museums", you will derive great enjoyment from the fascinating world of museums and galleries; there are some two thousand of them offering an immense variety and range of experiences so there is something for everyone. It is so exciting to feel the sense of exploring new areas in the world of museums and galleries. Make the most of what is on offer in 1989.

Sarah.

January 1989

EDITOR'S NOTE

This volume is one of a series of eleven regional guides to museums in the British Isles. The term 'museum' is often applied to a wide variety of collections and buildings: most of the places selected for description in the *Exploring Museums* guides, however, comply as far as possible with the Museums Association's definition of a museum as 'an institution that collects, documents, preserves, exhibits and interprets material evidence and associated information for the public benefit'.

Given the sheer quantity of museums in the British Isles, the guides describe only a selection, concentrating on those places that authors considered most worthy of a visit, either because of the quality of their collections and displays, or because of the interesting or unusual nature of what they have on view. Museums in each area not described in full are listed at the back of the guides, with brief details of their collections; please note that some of these are only open by appointment. The lists include new museums that are scheduled to open in the near future.

The principal aim of this series is to describe, through words and pictures, the types of things that visitors can expect to see and do at various museums. Authors have tried to put themselves in the shoes of a general museum visitor, and present a personal rather than an official view in their descriptions. It should be noted that specific items they describe may not be on show when you visit: most museums now change their displays fairly often, and if you want to see something in particular you should check beforehand with the museum concerned. Most of the illustrations have been selected by the authors, and highlight lesser-known objects and museum activities, as well as exhibits for which particular museums are renowned. Basic information about access and facilities has been kept to a minimum, as opening times or bus routes, for example, are frequently subject to change; please check with museums before visiting for precise details of opening times, holiday closures, admission prices, and how to get there, and for information on special events and activities.

Krystyna Matyjaszkiewicz
Series Editor

The views expressed in this guide are those of the author and not necessarily those of the Museums Association.

FOREWORD

President of the Museums Association
Patrick Boylan
and the Chairman of the Museums & Galleries Commission
Brian Morris

This series is being published in Museums Year 1989, which marks the centenary of the Museums Association. When the Association's first conference was held in York in 1889, there were already several hundred museums in Britain. Now there are some 2,300, and new ones are opening every month. They vary enormously in size and scope, from the large all-purpose museum to the small collection in a converted house. Many of the smaller museums are less well known than they should be, and it is these particularly that the books in this series seek to highlight.

Museums Year 1989, sponsored by The Times newspaper, represents the most significant promotion of the country's museums and galleries ever staged. Through their sponsorship Museums Year will bring fresh vitality to a particularly important part of our British heritage.

Never before have museums in general been as popular as they are today. In 1989 alone they are expected to receive between them something like 100 million visits (which is more than any sport or other leisure activity). They are especially attractive to young people, to the curious of all ages and to the lovers of beautiful, unusual and exciting things. There are indeed museums for every taste and interest, for every day and in every area. We are sure that these books will help many more people to discover the museums of Britain, to learn from them and to enjoy them.

INTRODUCTION

Good museums come in all shapes and sizes, but they do have one thing in common: they all have good collections. A museum may be exciting or relaxing, instructive, or just interesting; it may be housed in a palatial neo-classical building, an old factory, or a modern shed; but it will certainly have collections that can inspire the imagination, and can reach out to us from the past.

Swirling around every museum object are the phantoms of its owners and creators. When we gaze upon an object – whether it be the helmet of an ancient Greek warrior, a sampler lovingly embroidered by a young Victorian girl, or a Second World War ration book – we gaze directly through the mists of time. We may look back only a few years, several centuries or thousands of years to the days before human beings could write. Indeed, museums contain things that are older even than the human race. From the dawn of time come rocks and minerals, and from the later Triassic and Jurassic periods come dinosaurs. Such collections remind us that humans have inhabited this planet for the merest fraction of time.

Then there are the art galleries, where some of the most outstanding feats of cultural achievement can be found – paintings and sculptures that show the quest for understanding of ourselves and our environment.

Nowhere in Britain is as rich as the North East in museums and art galleries. The great cities of Bradford, Hull, Leeds, Newcastle and Sheffield all have superb collections, which are complemented and enhanced by those of an enormous variety of museums in town and country all over the region, from Grimsby, to Settle, to Berwick-upon-Tweed. There are museums to satisfy all tastes and curiosities, some well known and popular, others waiting to be discovered.

This great concentration of museums dates back over 150 years, to when learned societies in cities such as Leeds, Newcastle, Hull and York, and in towns like Scarborough, Whitby and Halifax, built up collections and created museums to house them. Museum development was not continuous, but more were gradually opened during the 19th century; **Sunderland**'s was the first municipal museum in the country. Many museums and galleries were based upon either private collections or bequests of money, often given to local authorities. The names of such benefactors live on in towns and cities all over the region – John Bowes (**Barnard Castle**), Walter Bagshaw (**Batley**), Joseph Shipley (**Gateshead**), T. R. Ferens (**Hull**), John and Albany Hancock, and Alexander Laing (**Newcastle**), J. N. and F. T. Mappin, and J. G. Graves (**Sheffield**) are just a few of them.

New museums have continued to be created throughout the 20th century. Great impetus has been provided in this region by the decline of industries, and industrial museums have blossomed in the wake of that decline, particularly in West Yorkshire. The growth of 'independent' museums during the 1970s and 1980s has been another important factor in the increase in numbers. Today, there are well over 300 museums in the North East.

To give some idea of the quality and diversity of museums and galleries in the area, I shall survey briefly the eight counties that make up the North East, mentioning some of the collections that there has not been room to describe more fully in this guide (but which are included in the list at the back).

Northumberland has the *Morpeth Chantry Bagpipe Museum*, where pipes and sound are combined in a most unusual way, and the *Thomas Bewick Birthplace Museum*, a celebration of the work of that great wood engraver. Then there are the Roman site museums near Hexham (*Chesters* and *Vindolanda*) and *Corbridge*. Tyne and Wear has its own Roman site, *Arbeia Roman Fort Museum*, still in the shadow of Hadrian's Wall, and the *John George Joicey Museum*, Newcastle, with its period settings, sporting guns, and models of the great flood (1771) and fire (1854). The *Durham Light Infantry Museum* flies the flag in County Durham for regimental museums, and shares premises with an Arts Centre; the *Darlington Railway Museum* boasts George Stephenson's world-famous locomotive, 'Locomotion'. In Cleveland, Hartlepool has the changing *Gray Art Gallery and Museum* and *Hartlepool Maritime Museum*, and Kirkleatham has its own developing museum at *Kirkleatham Old Hall*.

Into North Yorkshire, where life in the Pennine Dales is portrayed in Skipton's *Craven Museum*, the *Nidderdale Museum* in Pateley Bridge, and the *Upper Dales Folk Museum* in Hawes. In historic Richmond is the *Green Howards Museum*, and in even more historic Malton you can see the *Malton Museum*'s fine archaeology collections. Scarborough's *Rotunda Museum* is housed in a most wonderful building by the sea, while Harrogate's *Royal Pump Room Museum* is in what was once the town's best spa building. Among York's many attractions is the *Bar Convent Museum*, with its unique collections relating to the history of Christianity.

West Yorkshire alone has about fifty museums and galleries, and every town and city has at least one that is well worth visiting. The county's industrial past is saluted in the *Bradford Industrial Museum*, Halifax's *Calderdale Industrial Museum*, and the *Leeds Industrial Museum*, which has a good collection of locomotives as well as textile machinery. The declining coal industry is recalled 450ft underground in the *Yorkshire Mining Museum* at Caphouse Colliery. Important and varied collections are on view in the *Bankfield Museum*, Halifax, Huddersfield's *Tolson Museum*, *Leeds City Museum*, and *Wakefield City Museum*. *Pontefract Museum* is a splendid local museum, while the *Bronte Parsonage Museum* was once the home of the famous sisters, and houses some of the family's belongings. Unusual museums are to be found in Bradford (*Colour Museum*) and Holmfirth (*Holmfirth Postcard Museum*); another is the *Dewsbury Museum. Huddersfield Art Gallery* and the *Yorkshire Sculpture Park* offer contrasting views of art, the former housing Francis Bacon's important 'Figure Study II'.

Sheffield in South Yorkshire has many fine collections, ranging from art at the *Graves Art Gallery* and crafts at the *Ruskin Gallery*, to industrial material at *Sheffield Industrial Museum* and *Abbeydale Industrial Hamlet*. Barnsley has the *Cooper Gallery* and *Worsborough Mill Museum*, with its 17th century water-powered corn mill. *Doncaster Museum and Art Gallery* and *Rotherham Museum* both have diverse collections. In South Humberside, Grimsby's *Welholme Galleries* has good maritime holdings, and the *Baysgarth Museum* in Barton-on-Humber is developing a range of collections. On the North Bank, Hull's *Old Grammar School* is also expanding. More reclusive is the *University of Hull Art Collection*, strong in 20th century works. The *North Holderness Museum of Village Life* in Hornsea looks at changing life in the area, and Bridlington's *Sewerby Hall* has both archaeology and exhibits relating to the aviator, Amy Johnson.

Selecting places to describe in this guide from the region's treasure-house of museums and galleries has not been easy. I have tried to cover a range of subjects, types and sizes of museum, and readers should note that my personal choice will not be the same as that of anyone else! There is no such thing as a poor museum. All real museums – those with *real* collections – are of interest, and can stimulate and educate, however they may choose to present those collections.

Several times I have mentioned in descriptions that a museum is developing or expanding. Indeed, change is constant, and despite widespread funding difficulties, museums all over the North East are striving to offer new excitement and new challenges. Change also means that exhibits themselves change. If you ever visit a museum or gallery with the intention of seeing a particular object or group of objects, you must check with the museum in advance to establish whether or not what you wish to see is on view. Museums can never display all their collections all of the time because they do not have the space. Changes occur most frequently in art galleries, where the turnover of works on display can be very rapid. You have been warned!

Welcome to the magical world of museums in the North East!

David Fleming

ACKNOWLEDGEMENTS

Author's acknowledgements

I should like to record my thanks to the many friends and colleagues who have assisted and advised me in writing this guide, and who have provided me with information. Especially helpful have been Sue Underwood and Stephen Elson of the North of England Museums Service, and Ann Bukantas of the Ferens Art Gallery, Hull. I am grateful to Anne Lamb, Dorothy Soulsby, Jane Karlson and Pauline Greaves of Hull City Museums & Art Galleries for typing my manuscripts, and to Series Editor Krystyna Matyjaszkiewicz for her help and patience . . .

Photographic acknowledgements

The Museums Association is grateful to all the museums, archives and photographers who generously provided material for illustration herein, and to the copyright holders who wish to remain anonymous who kindly granted reproduction permission. Photographs were supplied by, and are reproduced courtesy of, the respective museums and their governing bodies or Trustees, except for those noted below.

Cover, detail of André Derain's *Barges on the Thames*, c.1906 (Leeds City Art Gallery) © copyright ADAGP Paris and DACS London 1989; colour plate 6, David Hockney's *Le Plongeur*, 1978 (Bradford Art Galleries and Museums) © copyright David Hockney 1978; pp. 3–4 (Barnsley), photographs by Cris Haigh, Sheffield; pp. 5–6 (Batley), and pp. 14–15 and Chair on cover (Birstall), © copyright and reproduced courtesy of Kirklees Libraries, Museums and Arts; pp. 23–24 (Durham Cathedral Treasury) © copyright and reproduced courtesy of The Dean and Chapter of Durham; p. 33 (Ferens Art Gallery), works by John Davies and Victor Newsome © copyright and reproduced courtesy of the artists; p. 45 (Jarrow), photograph of Bede's chair © copyright Archaeology Dept., University of Durham; p. 47 (Abbey House Museum), Doll conserved and photographed by North West Museum and Art Gallery Service; p. 50 (Leeds City Art Gallery), Francis Bacon's *Painting 1950* © copyright and reproduced courtesy of the artist; pp. 66–67 and Cameo on cover (Museum of Antiquities) © copyright and reproduced courtesy of the Museum of Antiquities of the University, Newcastle upon Tyne, and Society of Antiquaries of Newcastle upon Tyne; pp. 74–75 and half-title page (Bishops' House), and pp. 78–79 (Sheffield City Museum), © copyright and reproduced courtesy of Sheffield City Museums; pp. 76–77 reproduced courtesy of Sheffield City Art Galleries; p. 96 (York City Art Gallery), Paul Nash's *Winter Sea*, 1925–37 © copyright and reproduced courtesy of the Paul Nash Trust.

For Breton, Mitya, Callum, and for Sue.

Key to Symbols Used

F Free admission

£ Admission charge

V Voluntary donation requested

▣ Restaurant/cafeteria on premises

P Car Park on premises

♿ Good access and facilities for disabled

♿ Difficult/limited access and facilities for disabled and infirm

W Unstepped access via main or side door, wheelchair spaces, and adapted toilet

T Adapted toilet

X Flat or one-step access

A Access with 2–5 steps, or split level exhibition space

S Many unavoidable steps and/or other obstacles for wheelchair users and the infirm

G Provision made for guide dogs

(based on disabled access code devised by ARTSLINE (01 388 2227), the free telephone information service on the arts in Greater London for people with disabilities)

♦ Group visits

♦♦ School group visits

☺ Workshops/holiday events/guided tours/talks – 'phone for details

Museums shown in **bold** type in the text are described in full elsewhere in the volume; those shown in *italic* type are briefly described in the list of museums and collections at the back.

BARNARD CASTLE

The Bowes Museum

Barnard Castle, Co. Durham
DL12 8NP   (0833) 690606
Open daily. 🚻 💷 🅿
♿ W: steps to five rooms of
archaeology, otherwise all parts
easily accessible; parking close to
special entrance with intercom to
Reception; attendant help
available.
🚻 & 🚻 reduced admission for
groups of 10 or more; introductory
talks for 🚻 and teacher seminars
on request; Education Room for
schools, must be booked in
advance; contact Administrative
Officer. ☺

The Bowes is the most astonishing of
museums. It is enormous, purpose-
built as a museum late in the 19th
century, and looks like a French palace
transposed to the outskirts of the small
Teesdale market town of Barnard Castle.

Nor do the surprises end there, for
the building is crammed full of works
of decorative and fine art, most of them
continental, many of the highest quality. Both building and collections are
the legacy of John Bowes, son of the
10th Earl of Strathmore, and his
French wife, Josephine; they had the
museum built and amassed a collection
to fill it.

French decorative arts are predomi-
nant at the Bowes Museum. Furniture,
ceramics and tapestries are here in
glorious abundance. Beds with hang-
ings, bookcases, sofas, chairs, foot-
stools, cupboards, secretaires, chairs,
card tables, dining tables, sidetables,
dressing tables, commodes, sideboards
– every imaginable type of furniture
produced in France during the 18th
and 19th centuries, of the Louis XV,
Louis XVI, Directoire, Empire, and
Second Empire periods. The styles are
diverse, too, from extravagant Rococo,
to the refined and sophisticated Louis
XVI style, and the Romanticism of the

Second Empire (1852–70), by way of
the fantasy of Egyptian and Chinese
tastes. Outstanding among the French
furniture is a small writing desk
(*bonheur du jour*) of about 1770 by the
master cabinet maker, Martin Carlin,
veneered in tulip wood on oak with
plaques of Sèvres porcelain. Just as
good is the spectacular Warwick
Cabinet, actually an English cabinet
also made around 1770 to display a
panel of superb French marquetry of
the late 17th century.

French ceramics at the museum
principally feature the brilliantly coloured Sèvres porcelain, and the earlier
Vincennes porcelain. Other wares are
from St Cloud, Chantilly and Stras-
bourg. Again, this is a huge collection,
ranging from teapots to chamber pots.
Tapestries adorn the walls of the
French decorative art rooms. Among
these are the Psyche Tapestries, part of
a series telling the story of Cupid and
Psyche woven at Beauvais around
1670, perhaps for Louis XIV. Tarot
cards of about 1800, 18th century
illustrated books, and 17th century
painted enamels of Saints Ignatius
Loyola and Francis Xavier by Jacques
Laudin of Limoges are all worth looking out for.

Apart from French decorative art,

there is a great deal of material from
Britain and other European countries.
The museum's most famous exhibit is
undoubtedly the extraordinary Silver
Swan automaton of about 1770. This
originally came from the private
museum of a London goldsmith, and
after many adventures was bought by
John Bowes in 1872 for £200. When
operated, the lifesize swan moves its
neck, preens itself, and catches and
eats a fish in an eerily realistic performance. Other items of particular
note include some Dutch, French,
Russian and German ivories; a late
18th century Italian sedan chair; a set
of amber and clear table glass, probably
by the Bohemian Karl Pföhl; some
early 16th century Swiss choir stalls;
and English, Italian and Flemish furniture of the 16th to 18th centuries. Add
to this significant collections of silver,
clocks, textiles, costume, musical instruments and ceramics including
Meissen, Bow, Chelsea, and Chinese
porcelain, and you have a picture of the
richest collection of decorative art in
the North East.

As if all this weren't enough, there is
also the fine art – paintings, carvings,
and sculptures. The best carvings are
religious: 15th century English reliefs
in alabaster; an altarpiece of 1473–

Silver mechanical swan, made before 1773

The Warwick Cabinet, c.1770

Chelsea porcelain candlestick, c.1765

1500 depicting the Sufferings, Death and Resurrection of Christ; and a German limewood relief of the early 16th century with polychrome decoration, which is quite magnificent.

Religious subjects feature, too, in the museum's paintings. 'A Miracle of

the Holy Sacrament' (*c.* 1423–26) is by Sassetta, a major Sienese artist whose works show the new influences of the Renaissance, while Andrea Solario's 'St. Jerome in the Wilderness' (*c.* 1510–15) was painted in Milan under the influence of Leonardo da Vinci, high priest of the High Renaissance. The grisly 'Head of St John the Baptist' is a Flemish work from the studio of Dirck Bouts (*c.* 1415–75). Of about the same period is a triptych by the little-known Master of the *Virgo inter Virgines*, a Dutch artist active around 1470–1500. Somewhat later is the 'Christ appearing to the Apostles at the Sea of Galilee' by Maerten van Heemskerck (1498–1574), another Dutch painter, much influenced by Italian artists.

There is a second very fine painting by van Heemskerck, 'An Allegory of Innocence and Wisdom', with a dove and serpent to represent the two virtues. The 'Basket of Fruit' by Jacob van Hulsdonck (1582–1647) is a wonderful still life, matched almost by two other Flemish still lifes, these by Jan Pawel Gillemans the Younger. A contrast is offered by the 17th century Dutch and Flemish pictures of contemporary scenes. Cornelis Verbeeck's 'View on a Sea-Shore' has men,

women and children on the sands, with a vessel beaching and others out at sea. 'View on the Rhine' (1672) by Herman Saftleven is a landscape peopled by men, women, children and dogs, with a town and sailing vessels, all painted in acute detail, the sun breaking through the clouds to illuminate the whole.

French paintings in the Bowes include a dazzling 'Still Life' of 1642 by Jacques Linard, and two 19th century works – a 'Landscape with Cattle' by Jean Baptiste Camille Corot, and a 'Peasant Woman of Burgundy' that may be by Jean François Millet. There are few British paintings, but these are of high quality: from the 18th century a 'Portrait of a Lady' by Sir Joshua Reynolds and a painting of 'Elmsett Church' by Thomas Gainsborough, and from the 18th and 19th centuries watercolours by Thomas Girtin and J.M.W. Turner. A work of earlier date is the 'Portrait of a Lady' by Marcus Gheeraerts the Younger (*c.* 1561–1636), a Huguenot refugee to this country.

Four great old masters are represented, two of them Italian. Giovanni Battista Tiepolo painted 'The Harnessing of the Horses of the Sun' as an idea for a fresco in Milan, which sadly was destroyed in 1943. His 18th cen-

Jacob van Hulsdonck, A Basket of Fruit

El Greco, The Tears of St Peter, *c.1580–85*

BARNSLEY

Cannon Hall Museum

Cawthorne, Barnsley, South Yorkshire S75 4AT *(0226) 790270*
Open daily. 🄵 🄿
♿ **ST**: wheelchair access to ground floor only; some steps to negotiate there but staff on hand to assist if needed.
🚻 & 🍴 book in advance.

Not a town with the most glamorous image in Yorkshire, but Barnsley has a super country house museum just a few miles outside, in the village of Cawthorne. Extensive pottery collections and one of the best groups of Dutch paintings in the region are the main attractions, along with displays of English furniture, glassware, a regimental museum, gardens, a rolling country park of seventy acres, and Cannon Hall itself, a late 17th century building remodelled in the 18th century.

The art pottery on view by William Moorcroft, some of it made for Liberty & Co. of London, is exceptionally good (colour plate 11), and introduces a ceramic collection that contains a host of styles. I particularly liked among the Moorcroft pieces a flambé vase decorated with spring flowers of about 1952 by William's son, Walter. Other Liberty pottery includes a Gouda bowl made in Holland around 1905. Especially notable among further art pottery from the early years of this century are vases by Bernard Moore, a bowl and cover by Edmund Elton, and a cat by C.H. Brannan.

Burmantofts and Linthorpe pottery is vigorous and colourful. Somewhat later in date among displayed items are a red flambé penguin by Doulton (*c.* 1935), the figure 'Angela' by Leslie Harradine (1926; ill. on cover), and a powerful figure of a hound by Gilbert Bayes (*c.* 1930). Studio pottery by Bernard Leach and others, who returned to hand-making unique pieces, offers yet more contrasting shapes and designs.

Art nouveau and other late 19th to

Pottery Hound by Gilbert Bayes

early 20th century styles are prominent throughout the museum in pottery, metalware, furniture and glass. Continental art nouveau pewter of around 1900 is flamboyant and flowing, much of it again made for Liberty. English-made Liberty pewter from the turn of the century is equally attractive: trays, an inkwell, a centrepiece, a biscuit box, a delightful pewter-mounted liqueur decanter and glasses, and marvellous clocks. Liberty took the lead in the late 19th century revival of pewter-making, and, as in other design fields since then, their influence was very strong.

A superb art nouveau upholstered settee of around 1900 is another Liberty production. An art nouveau

tury contemporary, Antonio Canaletto, is best known for his views of his native Venice. Two excellent examples are in the Bowes Museum. The first is 'A Regatta on the Grand Canal', featuring a boat race with spectators in large ornamental boats, many wearing carnival costume. The second is 'The Bucintoro Returning to the Molo on Ascension Day', with the Doge's red and gold galley (*Bucintoro*) returning to the ducal palace. Both paintings are brimming with life and colour.

The Spaniard Francisco Goya painted the marvellous portrait of 'Don Juan Antonio Meléndez Valdes' and the 'Interior of a Prison', an almost monochrome study of profound feeling. Goya may also have painted the work called 'Portrait of the Painter's Brother (?)'. But perhaps the greatest painting in the museum, and an unqualified masterpiece, is 'The Tears of St. Peter' by the Cretan-born El Greco. This is the earliest of five versions of the subject, wherein Greco's intense religious passion is clear and eternal.

Smaller collections of archaeology, natural history, local history and toys are also on show at the Bowes Museum. But it is the decorative and fine art for which it is principally renowned, and that makes it one of the most exhilarating of all provincial museums.

Liberty art nouveau upholstered settee, c.1900

table, a form, chairs and a court cupboard, all in oak, show typical 17th century solidity. A more unusual item from the period is a laburnam-wood cabinet of about 1685. A large Brussels tapestry on display depicts 'The Judgement of Paris'. From the 18th century come fine gilt-framed mirrors, an English mahogany dining table, a massive Dutch walnut armoire, a mahogany secretaire bookcase, and a large glazed library bookcase, these last two containing a splendid collection of Chinese ivories.

The early 19th century furniture features some bizarre chairs with backs carved in the form of double eagles' heads, and an Egyptian-taste pedestal sideboard, complete with sham hieroglyphics. Two globes on display, one terrestrial and one celestial, are by J.

room setting in the museum includes an armchair (possibly Liberty), a copper inkwell with enamel decoration (*c.* 1900), and a display cabinet (1903) of mahogany inlaid with mother of pearl, pewter and stained woods, made by Cornelius Smith.

Beautiful glassware by René Lalique and Emile Gallé is of soaring quality. A 'Lovebirds' vase of about 1925 and a glass bird of about 1900 show the different approaches to form taken by Lalique, the leading art nouveau jeweller in Europe. Gallé's floral vase of about 1890, and two vases in the cameo technique show Gallé's brilliantly inspired and subtle skills. Other art nouveau pieces on display are by James Powell and Sons of London.

Many more periods, techniques and designs of glassware are represented in Cannon Hall's collections. The drinking glasses, for example, illustrate changes in style and manufacture from about 1650 onwards, a lovely Anglo-

Venetian glass incorporating white *latticino* decoration being the earliest of these. Salad bowls, fruit bowls, vases, decanters, lamps, candelabra and jugs are some of the creations in glass that show the incredible diversity and potential for beauty of this material. Especially interesting are the huge 'Queensland Vase' from the Val St Lambert factory in Belgium, a rare English glass hunting scene of about 1820, a glass house (complete with 'frozen' glass dog) of about 1880, Bohemian glass of the 19th century, and a remarkable window made entirely of tiny coloured glass beads. Modern Scandinavian glass is simple and effective, the pieces I like best being a bowl, 'Castello', designed by Helena Tynell, and a vase by the Orrefors Glass Company made in 1963.

Furniture and furnishings dating from the 17th to 19th centuries can be found all over the museum, and longcase clocks are also on show. A long

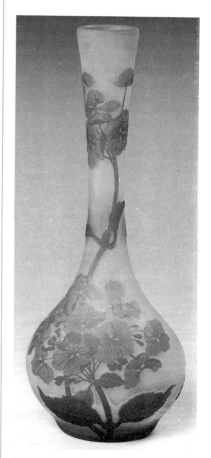

Floral vase by Emile Gallé, c.1890

and W. Carey and date from 1816. Later 19th century Arts and Crafts-style furniture continues this fascinating sequence of designs.

Cannon Hall has a wide range of excellent 17th century Dutch paintings. There are seascapes by masters in that field – 'A Calm' by William van de Velde, for example, and 'River Scene with Ships Becalmed' by Jan van der Capelle. Rich architectural detail features in pictures like 'The House in the Wood' by Jan van der Heyden, while minute observation characterises 'Fruit and Insects' by Abraham Mignon, wherein insects, snails and a caterpillar attack decaying fruit – a favourite subject among still-life painters of the time. 'Landscape with Tower and Figures by a Lake' by Jan Both and 'Ponte Rotto, near Rome' by Jan Asselijn are landscapes by Dutch artists who were heavily influenced by the Italian style. 'Child Holding an Apple' is a charming study by Caesar van Everdingen, and there are other portraits, such as 'A Peasant Filling his Pipe' and 'A Woman Drinking' by Adriaen van Ostade.

There is also a wide variety of other items at Cannon Hall. Among these is a model showing changes in coal mining through the ages, appropriate since Barnsley lies at the centre of an important mining area. This is accompanied by details of mining disasters, such as the one at Silkstone Colliery in 1838 when twenty-six children died, the girls aged between eight and seventeen, the boys between seven and ten years old; at Oaks Colliery in 1866 341 men were killed. On a lighter note are toys, dolls, samplers and costume.

In addition, Cannon Hall houses the Lillywhite Museum, with collections relating to the 13/18th Royal Hussars (Queen Mary's Own) Regiment. Both of the two original regiments took part in many major military campaigns, and the 13th Light Dragoons formed part of the Charge of the Light Brigade at the Battle of Balaclava in 1854. Relics of this action include a sabre, and the shako (a type of helmet) worn by Cornet Denzil Thomas Chamberlayne, whose horse, Pimento, was killed under him.

BATLEY

Bagshaw Museum

Wilton Park, Batley, West Yorkshire WF17 OAS   (0924) 472514
Open daily. 🅵 🅿
♿ **S**: wheelchair access to ground floor only.
🚻 & 🚻 book in advance with Curator.

Walk through Wilton Park in Batley on a stormy night, and you will come upon a Victorian Gothic house straight out of a Hammer film. Go there during the day, and you will discover a museum that houses unexpected treasures.

Bagshaw Museum dates back to 1911, when Walter Bagshaw opened to the public three rooms of 'The Woodlands', a house owned by Batley Corporation. On view were textiles, and items of biblical history and natural history, donated by local people. Some of these original collections are on display today in the Bagshaw Room.

The collections grew over the years, and now fill the house and stores.

Objects given by the Bagshaw family themselves include beadwork purses of the 1890s, beaded handbags, Eskimo items such as a fish-hook and a pipe of walrus ivory, and a Yukon-territory sheep-bone bowl and spoon. A relative of the Bagshaws donated objects from Chinese Ming dynasty tombs, some of which are still wrapped in the handkerchief in which he gave them. A picture of flowers, bought at a Church bazaar on the Balmoral estate, is reported to have been painted by Princess Alix, who became Tsarina of Russia.

The Bagshaw Room also contains a shell collection in its original drawers, boxes and jars. A stalked crinoid (sea lily), a common prawn, and a Portuguese Man-o'-War float sadly in their spirit jars. There are seeds of turnip, hemlock, soya bean and henbane, and specimens showing the life history of the bee and the metamorphosis of the silkworm. A Crown of Thorns, Jewish Torah (Roll of the Law), Tallith (prayer shawl) and Phylacteries (small leather boxes containing Hebrew texts)

Jewish Crown of Thorns, Torah, Tallith and Phylacteries

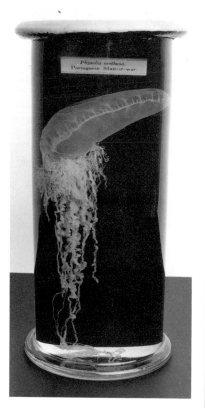

Portugese Man-o'-War

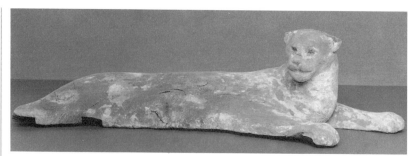

Ancient Egyptian wooden cat

Chinese Shou Lao figure

were all on show at the opening of the museum in 1911. Another inhabitant of the Bagshaw Room is a bronze statue of a miner, entitled 'The Dignity of Labour'.

The dining room of the house has a floor, walls and ceiling of oak, with an unusual painted frieze showing imaginary Medieval scenes of ploughing, sowing, harvesting, threshing and hunting. The room contains a veritable miscellany of exhibits: pottery; kitchen equipment; gentlemen's costume accessories (neckties, cravats, hats) and day-to-day necessities (hat-stretcher, match strikers, sovereign case, snuff boxes, tie press, boot jacks, razor); and model vehicles. Among the latter is one of a horsedrawn tram of the Dewsbury, Batley & Birstall Tramway Company Ltd, formed in 1873. Two model vehi-

cles are pulled by horses, one of them scruffy and endearing, the other being reined in so hard by its clown driver that all four feet have left the ground! In another case stands the plaster model for a statue of locally-born Joseph Priestley, discoverer of oxygen (he called it 'dephlogisticated air').

Cigarette cards from Player's and Ogden's make a colourful display. A cycle set features Sawyer's Velocipede, the 'Invincible' Tandem tricycle, and the Family tandem with sidecar. A sea set illustrates 'Hanno the Carthaginian', 'Mutiny on the "Dreadnought"'

(which has the captain pointing his gun at the mutinous crew), and 'Pirates decoying an American Ship' (where the pirates are disguised as women).

Necklaces of red carnelian, various stones, and blue faience, one decorated with Eye of Horus amulets, along with bracelets and rings, introduce visitors to the Ancient Egyptian collections, a mysterious world seemingly obsessed with death and the hereafter. A grave marker, coloured with greens and reds, carries an inscription to a lady TA-BAKT-EN-MUT. Painted mummy masks show how the Egyptians tried to preserve the appearance of the dead. The dead themselves are here too, if only in the shape of a single mummified leg attached to a full-size reconstructed mummy. There are canopic jars, which were used to store internal organs of the dead, and a canopic chest of 664–325 BC bearing a painting of Anubis (jackal-headed guardian god of the cemetery) and inscribed 'he who is continually happy'. Further items buried with the dead include model horses to provide transport in the afterlife, and a model palm tree to provide shade and oil.

A range of other objects is more readily associated with life, rather than death, in Ancient Egypt: bowls and vases of white argonite, pottery over 5,000 years old, adzes, axes, a stone loom weight, and wooden mallets used by stone masons. There is 'djed' pillar, which probably represents a tree with its branches lopped off, and was used originally in agricultural and fertility rituals to signify rebirth. Linen cloth, a basket fragment from Deir-el-Bahari, a plaited leather girdle from Quarara, a writing tablet, and reed pens all bring to life Egyptian people and their work. A hand mirror of 663-525 BC, kohl pots (for kohl or galena, a black lead ore used as eye liner), a slate palette to hold unguents and perfumes of about 1580 BC, and a slate palette for grinding cosmetic powders of the same date remind us of the eternal nature of vanity. A plaster headrest was even used as a pillow to prevent elaborate Egyptian hairstyles from being crushed! The star exhibit among the Egyptiana is a wooden cat with a body like a seal.

The Chinese collection explodes with brilliant colour and ornament. A Confucius figure robed in Imperial Yellow, altar lions (the Dog of Fo), a figure of Shou Lao, god of longevity, and roof ridge-tiles in the shape of an actor, a carp and a grotesque, are powerful ceramic images in the vigorous Chinese style. Other pottery includes some beautiful vases, one representing a double-faced god with a head open to receive written prayers, another a pear-shaped 'Devil's Work' vase with images of the K'ang-Hsi period, 1662-1772. A ceramic garden shrine has Shou Lao standing by a peach tree with a fishpond below him.

Among the Chinese jade is a Ming (1368–1644) box in the shape of a tortoise, a symbol of the North and of water. In ancient times all tortoises were believed to be female, and were thought to mate with snakes. A Ming bronze bowl is supported by three legs in the form of elephant heads. Another Ming elephant carries on its back a symbolic vase of heavenly dew, poured by the gods on the world to calm troubles.

In the Chinese room is arguably the best museum display case in the region, which along with stimulating natural history displays, the 1643 seige at Howley Hall (in models and cork), and the lovely wooded Wilton Park, makes a visit to Bagshaw Museum a must. Oh, and if you're interested in astronomy, do have a peer through the four inch refracting and the fifteen inch reflecting telescopes in the Milner K. Ford Observatory, in the park.

BEAMISH

Beamish, The North of England Open Air Museum

Beamish, Co. Durham DH9 ORG
(0207) 231811
Closed Mondays from November to March. 🔊 🖵 🅿
♿ ST: extensive site, not ideal for wheelchair-bound.
🚻 & ♦ book in advance: contact Bookings Officer; events programme available. ☺

Beamish Museum, where 'The Past is Brought to Life Again', is a remarkable achievement. It is the open air museum that looks at life in the whole of the North East region, largely in the early part of this century. Its collections are immense and diverse, it is developing continuously, and it is a popular family museum.

The entrance to the 260 acre site (which is a difficult area to cover for

wheelchair users) is under 'Tiny Tim', a 70 ton steam hammer, built in 1883, of a type used in making wrought iron forgings, especially in shipbuilding. The Visitor Centre has a taste of things to come in its display of enamel signs advertising a great number of products most of which are no longer available. If you wonder where today's television advertisers get some of their imaginative ideas, look no further – the imagery in these enamels can be quite fantastic, and totally unrelated to what they are advertising. (Sounds familiar ?)

Once on site, Beamish is divided into areas that illustrate different themes. These areas are linked by footpaths, by road and by a tramway, and visitors have the choice of walking from one area to another, or catching a bus or tramcar. Several electric tramcars are working at the moment, including a Gateshead No.10 single-deck tramcar, over 60 years old, a Sheffield No.264 double-decker tramcar, over 70 years old, and a 1902 Blackpool tramcar (colour plate 10). Instant nostalgia for those old enough to remember.

Industry in the North East was based on the coalfields, and Beamish is re-creating a colliery as it might have

Terrace of Georgian houses in the Old Town Street at Beamish

appeared in about 1913. Although virtually all the buildings and other features at Beamish have been brought to the museum from elsewhere, there is a genuine drift mine on the site, known as Mahogany Drift. Drift mines were shallow tunnels dug to extract coal from seams lying near the surface. Closed in 1958, visitors can now go down Mahogany Drift to get some idea of what working conditions were like in such a mine.

The colliery has an engine house with a working steam winding engine, built in 1855 by J. and G. Joicey and Company of Newcastle for the Beamish Colliery, close by the museum. A boiler house, a heapstead (or building where coal was sorted and cleaned), a powder house and an engine shed can also be seen. The engine shed houses the Hetton Colliery locomotive, built in 1822 by George Stephenson; it is one of the world's oldest locomotives. Nearby is a row of miners' cottages, brought here from Hetton-le-Hole. The cottages were built originally in the 1860s, and were occupied by miners' families until 1976. They are furnished to show the lifestyle of pitmen and their families prior to the First World War, and are full of period furniture, fittings, ornaments and household equipment.

The largest exhibit at Beamish is a 100 ton steam navvy, built in Lincoln in 1931. It is part of a miscellaneous transport collection, which includes the aforementioned working tramcars. There are two steam road rollers, one of them the 'Astonisher', built by John Fowler and Company in Leeds in 1925, and used in Gosforth, the other an Aveling and Porter model. A Foster portable steam engine awaits restoration. Inside the transport shed is a laundry van and an 'Open Lot' gipsy caravan (*c.*1900). Motorcycles, a trolley-bus, a 1925 Austin hearse, and an hermaphrodite sleigh (convertible to wheels) are other vehicles to be seen.

The Home Farm is the second main feature at Beamish that was there before the museum. In a farmstead whose layout has changed little since the 1790s, the museum keeps poultry, pigs, sheep, cattle, and a thriving col-

Inside the Co-op grocery shop in the Old Town Street

Traditional farmhouse at Home Farm

ony of farmyard cats. The stars among the livestock are the Shorthorn cattle. Once Britain's major dual-purpose breed (reared for both dairy produce and meat), the Shorthorn was overwhelmed this century by imported breeds such as the familiar black and white Friesian. Beamish's Shorthorns include two bulls, and a breeding operation is under way, which is very fitting as Shorthorns were originally bred in County Durham.

As well as the animals, Home Farm has a collection of farm implements,

large and small. The best part of the farm is the restored and refurnished farmhouse, which is a triumph of period reconstruction. Settle yourself into a rocking-chair by the fire, and ZZZ . . .

Beamish has plans to operate its other farm, Pockerley Farm, as a mixed farm of around 1914, using horses.

A country railway station has been created at Beamish, with bridges and buildings that have been brought together from various places. The passenger station building itself came from the village of Rowley, where it was constructed in 1867. That station never had gas or electricity, only oil. Other buildings include a goods shed and office, a weigh cabin, a signal box from Carr House East, Consett, and 'cells' used for coal and lime storage. The station has coal and goods wagons, a steam locomotive from Hetton Colliery of 1914, and a North Eastern Railway class 'C' steam locomotive built at Gateshead in 1889, which is the sole survivor of a class of 200 engines. There is also a replica of George Stephenson's famous

'Locomotion', the first locomotive built for a public railway, the Stockton and Darlington Railway, in 1825; it can often be seen in steam.

The most popular part of Beamish now is the 'Town', a series of buildings furnished to represent life in a North East market town in the early part of the century. There is a park with bandstand, a pub with brewery horses in the stables, a Co-op, a stationer's shop, and a row of fashionable terraced Georgian houses containing the business and domestic premises of a solicitor, a dentist and a music teacher.

The Co-op – actually a reconstruct-

NER class C locomotive at the station

ion of the Annfield Plain Industrial Co-operative Society store – houses a drapery, grocery and hardware departments. Those were the days of personal service, when you could buy goods that were not all pre-packed, when cash moved around a shop on overhead wires (or in tubes), and when nobody had ever thought of 'eat-by' dates! Of course, life expectancy was not as long . . .

Like the pub, the Co-op and the stationer's, the terraced houses are full of period fittings and furnishings. The dentist's house has its surgery upstairs, arranged around a cast-iron dental chair and treadle drill, with gas cylinders to hand. The technician's room, with its dentures and accoutrements, is next door. The rest of the house has middle-class furnishings, complete with William Morris and Charles Voysey wallpaper designs, and Shanks bath and shower unit.

Beamish is a nationally important museum whose collections recall a wealth of experience in the North East. The range of its household and commercial collections, in particular, is almost unrivalled. The scale of the museum is huge, and it is still growing.

Bedroom of the Dentist's House, Ravensworth Terrace, Beamish

BERWICK-UPON-TWEED

Berwick-upon-Tweed Borough Museum and Art Gallery

The Clock Block, Berwick Barracks, Berwick-upon-Tweed, Northumberland TD15 1DG
(0289) 330933
Open daily. ▣ (joint admission with KOSB Regimental Museum)
♿ S: wheelchair access limited.

The historic and beautiful border town of Berwick-upon-Tweed is the home of two notable museums, both housed in Britain's first purpose-built barracks (begun in 1717).

Adjacent to the **King's Own Scottish Borderers Regimental Museum** (see below), to which there is a joint admission charge, is Berwick Borough Council's own museum, which is currently being redeveloped. The local history displays look at aspects of life in the town, and feature in particular salmon fishing, with a fording-box or lookout post for salmon, and a salmon coble, or flat-bottomed fishing boat.

What makes this a museum of outstanding interest, however, are the displays of fine and decorative art donated to Berwick by Sir William Burrell, better known as benefactor of the city of Glasgow, where the famous Burrell Collection is now on view. Berwick's own Burrell collection is smaller in scale, but contains some wonderful items. Especially beautiful are the Japanese and Chinese ceramics, including superb Japanese Imari ware dishes and Chinese tiles of the K'ang Hsi period (1662–1722). A drawing of 'Russian Dancers' by that masterly 19th century artist, Edgar Degas, in charcoal and pastel on tinted paper, is one of a splendid collection of paintings and drawings. Other favourites of mine are a Dutch 17th century 'Still

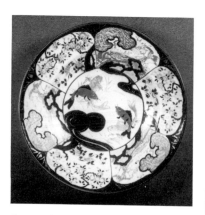

Japanese Imari Ware dish

Edgar Degas, Russian Dancers

The King's Own Scottish Borderers Regimental Museum

The Barracks, Berwick-upon-Tweed,
Northumberland TD15 1DG
(0289) 307426
Open daily. ⚅ (joint admission with
Borough M&AG)
♿ S: wheelchair access limited.
🚻 & 🚻 book in advance.

The King's Own Scottish Borderers
Regiment (K.O.S.B.) has a long history, having first been raised in Edinburgh in 1689 by the Earl of Leven.
Unofficially, it was known at first as the
Edinburgh Regiment. Its large and
varied collections give us many insights
into the forging of the British Empire,
and the horrifying conflicts of the 20th
century, up to and including the Falklands War. Behind the bright red and
tartan uniforms, the sinister bayonets,
rifles, revolvers and machine guns, and
the glittering medals, stand the shades
of thousands of men killed fighting in
scores of battles on foreign soil because
politicians could find no better way of
resolving their differences.

Indeed, what greets that visitor on
entering the museum is a list of the
engagements and campaigns that have
involved the K.O.S.B.: Namur 1695;
Afghanistan 1878–80; South Africa
1900–02; the dread names of Mons,
Ypres, Loos, Somme and Arras; and
Dunkirk, Arnhem and Korea. Nearby
is a stencilled board reading 'Dont

Vickers .303 machine-gun

hamg [*sic*] about here you may not be
killed. Others will be.' As if to confirm
this message, there are the medals of
Pipe Majors Laurie and Mackenzie.
Both had retired from the Army before
the First World War, but both volunteered again during that conflict, and
were killed at the Battle of Loos,
Mackenzie aged sixty. In all, nearly
7,000 men of the regiment were killed
during that terrible war, and the
museum displays the brass plaque
erected by the men of the K.O.S.B. in
memory of their comrades, brought
inside before it was completely worn
away by daily polishing.

The museum has a room devoted to
medals, including six Victoria Crosses
with their simple inscription 'For
Valour'. One of these was awarded to
C.S.M. J. Skinner in September 1917;
six months later he was killed by a
sniper at Passchendaele. There are
German medals, too, one an Iron
Cross belonging to General von Kap-
pel, which was captured from his room
by the K.O.S.B. in 1917.

The weaponry on display is impressive in its range and ferocity. While
firearms are often decorative, bayonets,
daggers and swords look as deadly as
they were intended to be. A German
saw-edged bayonet is the nastiest blade
on view, although two German daggers
– one inscribed *Alles für Deutschland*,
the other an S.S. dagger inscribed
Meine Ehre Heist Treue (My Honour is
True) – are more chilling.

British rifles include a short .303
Martini Henry cavalry carbine, a .303
short magazine Lee Enfield rifle, and a
flintlock Brown Bess made by the
Tower Armouries in the 18th century.
There are a number of machine-guns,
the most fearsome of which is a Vickers
.303. This was first introduced into the
K.O.S.B. in 1897 as the Maxim, later
to be issued as the Vickers, and stayed
in service virtually unchanged until
1964. On open display – in the middle
of the floor! – is a Russian light
machine-gun captured from the
Chinese by 'D' Company of the 1st
Battalion in 1951. Perhaps the
strangest exhibit among the weaponry
is a Thompson submachine-gun, be-
loved of the Chicago Prohibition-

Life' by Philips Angel, 'The Bugler' by
James Maris, and the late 19th century
'Snow Scene – Railway Station' by
Henry Muhrman.

The displays of the Burrell collection change, but the quality is eternal,
and Berwick is fortunate in having such
magnificent pieces. Together with the
intelligent local history displays at Berwick Museum, and the **K.O.S.B. Regimental Museum**'s collections, the
Burrell items make up a concentration
of historic material that is probably
unrivalled in a town of this size.

Ram's Head snuff mull of the 1st Battalion (K.O.S.B. Regimental Museum)

BEVERLEY

Museum of Army Transport

Flemingate, Beverley, North Humberside HU17 0NG
(0482) 860445
Open daily. 🚻 ▣ 🅿
♿ W: wheelchair access to all areas except Beverley Aircraft and the Bar.
🚹 & 🚻 must book at least 24 hours in advance: contact Museum Manager. ◎

period gangsters, presented to the K.O.S.B. by the Provisional IRA in 1985. Another case has weapons confiscated by the 1st Battalion in Northern Ireland during 1969–76, including Colt, Webley, and Smith & Wesson revolvers.

Weapons of a different culture are the souvenirs of campaigns in Africa, such as the spears taken from the 'Kaffir Chief Tatto', who was killed in battle during the Bechuanaland War in 1897. Other spoils from Africa include a Dervish tunic and sword, seized during the campaign against the Mahdi and his followers in Sudan in the 1880s. These trophies are complemented by gifts, received in Borneo and Sarawak in 1966, of a totem pole, and Iban knives, blow-pipe and darts.

The uniforms are many and various, and are constant reminders of the Scottish nature of the regiment. They range from buttons and badges, to helmets, hats, tam o'shanters, glengarries and shakos, to full dress uniform, and to battledress as worn in the jungles of Malaya and Borneo. Pride of place goes to the uniform of Field Marshal Earl Haig, Commander-in-Chief of the British armies in France during the First World War, and Col-

onel of the K.O.S.B. from 1923–28.

The rest of the museum's extensive collections comprise the general miscellany that is associated with soldiers and warfare. At one extreme are items such as a blood-stained field-dressing, a piece of the first parachute dropped at Arnhem, and a water-bottle with bullet holes. Then there are the twenty-four-hour ration packs (nowadays containing, for example, powdered oxtail soup, apple and apricot flakes, boiled sweets, and baconburgers), the model and Ensign of H.M.S. Berwick, and a drum of 1796 carried at the Battle of Alexandria in 1801. And at the other extreme is the regimental silver, which boasts an ornamental emu egg, and an enormous ram's head snuff mull of the 1st Battalion.

Add to all this the maps, photographs and drawings, and you have one of the best regimental collections in the North. A laconic museum caption caught my eye, summing up a little of the horror, the heroism and the ultimate futility of war, in a comment upon one method of defence against gas warfare in the First World War – a length of rifle-cleaning cloth wetted and tied around the face: 'It did not work very well'.

Tanks, locomotives, staff cars, motorcycles, horsedrawn wagons, trucks, aircraft – this museum has the lot. Sited most unexpectedly in the shadow of the glorious Beverley Minster, the museum deals with all aspects of moving armies and their supplies, and displays some of the most spectacular exhibits in the region, as well as some of the strangest.

The largest of these is the Blackburn 'Beverley', an enormous silver transport aircraft built in 1955 for carrying heavy loads and for short hauls. Having gone out of service in 1974, the 'Beverley' survived an attempt to turn it into a nightclub before finding the haven of the museum. This type of aircraft was popular with pilots, despite its great girth, and was a familiar sight in Aden and the Gulf states during the 1960s. A second aeroplane at Beverley is the small De Havilland 'Beaver', used in liaison and reconnaissance since the 1960s, from Borneo to Belfast.

Next in size after the 'Beverley' are the locomotives, although one, the toytown 'Gazelle' built in 1896, is supposed to be the smallest loco ever to have operated on standard gauge railways in this country. Railways have been important for army transport since the mid-19th century, as the French found to their cost during the 1870 Franco-Prussian War. 'Woolmer' spent over forty years in service, being retired in 1954. This small loco is displayed hauling a RECTANK flat

Blackburn Beverley transport aircraft, built in 1955

wagon of the First World War period. An armoured train vehicle of 1915 still awaits its 12-pounder gun, but demonstrates the type of conversion of ordinary rolling stock common during the First World War. A second armoured rail vehicle of the same period is the 40 hp armoured Simplex rail tractor, built to haul trains of ammunition and supplies to the front in France and Flanders.

The loco 'Rorke's Drift', an early diesel shunter of 1933, was requisitioned by the army during the Second World War. The 'Warwell' is a wagon built to carry armoured vehicles of up to fifty tons during the war. A German rail wrecker, or rooter, is an extraordinary device built by the Wehrmacht to destroy railways ahead of the Allied advance. The one on display was captured in Italy.

Two shunting locos, the diesel Army 110 and the steam loco 'Waggoner' both of the 1950s, bring the story of military railways more up to date, while a large number of smaller railway exhibits – Persian railway insignia, the wine list of the 10,000th British Berlin Military Train, and workshop equipment, for example – fill out the tale.

Then there are the tanks, in many ways the most brutal of weaponry, massively heavy, and thunderously powerful. A Crusader Mark 1 tank was recovered from a live firing range to be displayed in the museum as a casualty. A Charioteer FV4101 tank is actually a Cromwell tank converted in the 1950s to carry a 20-pounder gun. A Comet

Charioteer tank

Mark lb tank was in service from 1945 to 1960, used for trials at the Fighting Vehicles Research and Development Establishment.

Tank transporters, not surprisingly, are even bigger than tanks, and are among the mightiest of all road vehicles. The largest of these at the museum is the British Thorneycroft 'Antar' Mark 1B, powered by a Rolls Royce 'Meteorite' engine. Just as impressive is the American Diamond T Model 980, also with a Rolls Royce engine. This vehicle entered the theatre of war for the first time in the battles of the North African desert campaign during the Second World War.

Smaller vehicles are here by the score. The horsedrawn GS wagon Mark XI is a remnant of earlier days, but was still used widely on the battlefields of the Western Front during the First World War. Not so widely used was the ungainly wheelbarrow, employed by Chinese labour gangs in France. It looks more like a spinning wheel than a vehicle.

Between the two World Wars mechanisation of transport proceeded rapidly, and all sorts of specialised and

Antar tank transporter

SAS Pink Panther

general purpose vehicles emerged. Among these were the Morris Commercial 'D' type 30 cwt truck of 1926, the Morris 8 cwt truck, the Talbot AV75 ambulance of 1936 (only three of which survive), and a most unusual three-wheeled motorcycle, based on a Triumph 500 SV Model 'P' Mark 2.

The Second World War produced hosts of vehicles for different purposes and various terrains. The 'Universal' carrier, better known as the Bren Gun Carrier, is a classic war vehicle of which nearly 50,000 were built in Britain and Canada. The 'Dingo' scout car, armed with its .303 Bren gun, and the Daimler armoured car Mark 1 with its 2-pounder gun, are two light armoured vehicles that saw a great deal of action. The half-track M14 armoured personnel carrier was popular for desert warfare. The 'Jeep', a Ford GPW ¼ ton light transport vehicle, probably became the most familiar Second World War vehicle of all, over 600,000 being built by the end of the war.

Of the same vintage is a transportable field bakery, used during the War to provide fresh bread for troops at the front. The museum's bakery was used in Cyprus into the 1980s, before being retired. Unexpectedly, it saw further service in the Falklands War, producing over 270,000 loaves during an eight-month period.

Post-war development continued, leading to curiosities such as the

Hunting-Percival 'Harrier', a completely folding vehicle of 1957, designed for parachute drops. Rather more obvious is the TV1000 'Rhino', an experimental wheeled cross-country vehicle powered by a 533 bhp 'Meteorite' engine, and the only one ever built.

Other military vehicles of special note include the Pink Panther (a pink Land Rover used by the SAS in desert duties), a SRN 6 Mark 2 hovercraft, a landing Vehicle Mark 3, and the DUKW, an unarmoured amphibious

vehicle designed in 1942. During the first four months after the invasion of Europe in 1944 DUKWs carried 40 per cent of all supplies landed.

A group of staff cars shows that the hardships endured by the ordinary troops are not all that there is to life in the army. Two Humbers, a Rover and a Daimler, all black and chrome, testify to the privileges of rank, but Field Marshall Montgomery's 1939 Rolls Royce 'Wraith' outshines them all. Improbably, the 'Wraith' was landed on 'Juno' beach just after D-Day, and remained in Europe for the rest of the war. Rather more reassuring is the Humber 'Super Snipe' touring car, now in camouflage livery, used by Montgomery in Italy.

Should clambering over the specially-designated 'Explore' vehicles inside the museum not be enough for you (just try 'driving' the Pig, for example) there is a Junior Assault Course outside, complete with Churchill tank. Go on the right day and you will also see demonstrations (these generally take place on the last Sunday in May, June, July and August, and Bank Holiday Mondays in May and August). If you think you don't like military museums, this one might just surprise you.

Field Marshall Montgomery's 1939 Rolls Royce Wraith

BIRSTALL

Oakwell Hall and Country Park

Nutter Lane, Birstall, Nr Batley, West Yorkshire WF17 9LG
(0924) 474926
Open daily. **F ◼ P**
&. **ST**: wheelchair access to ground floor only (Hall, gardens, wildlife garden, shop, cafe, craft workshop and events barn); staff will give any necessary assistance on request.
🚻 should book in advance: contact Administrative Assistant; unbooked groups may not be admitted to Hall at busy periods.
🚻 must book in advance: contact Assistant Curator, Education; unbooked groups will not be admitted to Hall or educational facilities. 17th century 'Living History' Costume Days for schools on Mondays during term time: advance booking essential. ☺

Built in 1583 by John Batt, Oakwell Hall is a superb stone-built manor house, which retains a medieval layout, and is set in an eighty-seven acre country park. The house is being re-furnished faithfully according to how it would have been in the 17th century, and it creates a sense of that period most successfully.

This sense of the past begins in the Herb Garden, with its agrimony, lung-wort, catmint, Lady's Mantle, Lady's Bed Straw, feverfew and damask rose. The garden is laid out on a traditional 17th century geometric pattern. Herbs were very commonly used in the 17th century in medicine and cooking, and for their scents.

The Kitchen leads directly onto the garden. It has a stone floor and large fireplace, and contains pine prepara-tion tables, cooking implements of all kinds, such as pestle and mortar, toast-ers, and pots and pans, and an oak settle. This reconstruction of a 17th

Exterior view of Oakwell Hall

century kitchen, featuring a range of reproduction earthenware, is really quite exceptional.

The Great Hall was essentially a reception room in the time of John Batt and his son Robert, and was simply furnished. The floor is stone-flagged, the walls are panelled in oak, and the mullioned and leaded windows give timeless views of the park through their ancient glass. Dog gates at the foot of the staircase to the gallery are an un-common survival of a feature designed to prevent the household dogs from slinking upstairs. The fireplace con-tains a cast-iron patterned fireback. The main items of furniture are oak chairs, an elaborately carved settle, and an early 17th century long table, which is decorated with a frieze of dragons.

The Great Parlour was the principal living room in the 17th century. It contains an oak gateleg table, chairs, a longcase clock, and other furniture, all set on woven rush matting. The win-dow recesses carry plaster decorations, but the most important feature in the room is the remarkable painted panell-ing, a rare surviving example of this type of decoration. Above the fireplace is a painted landscape.

The third main living room on the ground floor is the Little Parlour in the east wing. This contains another long table, and chairs, one a typical Yorkshire-style chair with carved lozenge design and decorative crest, as well as a fine court cupboard. There

Dog gates in the Great Hall

are also appropriate portraits, ceramics and glassware.

Upstairs, the panelled Great Parlour Chamber has a concealed lavatory, a tester bed, chest of drawers, gateleg table and chairs, with personal items dotted around, such as a clay pipe, money, weights, hat, book, bottle and glass. The Buttery Chamber displays a group of late 17th century chairs, showing a diversity of carvings. One of them has been stripped entirely of numerous layers of ancient varnish to reveal an inlay pattern.

The Painted Chamber, like the

The Great Parlour, Oakwell Hall, with 17th century painted wall panelling

Great Parlour, has splendid painted panelling, which creates a three-dimensional effect. Reproduction furniture shows the glorious honey colour of oak unstained by varnish or woodsmoke. Nearby, the intimate Study looks onto the gallery of the Great Hall. It contains a writing desk, pewter ink pot, spectacles and books, and is a charming little room.

Maps of Yorkshire and the West Riding adorn the green panelled walls of the Green Chamber, seen here in its 18th century form. These include maps by John Speed of 1610, Richard Blome of 1670, and J. Cary of 1809. The Porch Chamber has been restored to give views of the roof construction of the house. Set into the floorboards is a display that contains various items found in the house during the restoration work of 1986–88, such as combs, wooden knitting needles, and an exercise book. The last recalls the use of the house as a girls' boarding school in the 19th century. It was during this time that Charlotte Brontë wrote *Shirley*, the heroine of which lived in Fieldhead, which is actually a thinly-disguised Oakwell Hall.

A meal ark for storing food, some chests, a cupboard, and a truckle bed are to be found what is known as the Kitchen Chamber, along with armour, a crossbow, a saddle, a horn lantern and pottery. This was probably a servants' chamber or store room, and has plain plastered walls. The bed, a reproduction, is on wheels, as the original was designed to be wheeled under larger beds for storage.

The Little Parlour Chamber has its own *en suite* dressing room, and contains a cradle, a table, and the Westmoreland Bed of about 1525. The bed is carved ornately with monsters, flowers, the Lamb of God, the Tree of Life, and other designs. Occupants were instructed by inscriptions to 'Drede God', 'Love God' and 'Prayes God'. The chamber and dressing room contain reproduction 17th century costume (very little original costume from that date survives), and once more the period feel is extremely well conveyed.

Various events, special activities and exhibitions, many held in the farm buildings on the estate, help visitors enter the spirit of the age. Literally a stone's throw from the M62, Oakwell Hall, with its gardens and park, is a delightful place to visit. It will reward you with a true sense of the lives of 17th century gentlefolk.

BRADFORD

Bolling Hall

Bowling Hall Road, Bradford, West Yorkshire BD4 7DP (0274) 493313
Open daily. 🇫 🅿
♿ S: disabled access available from rear of building to 18th century wing and housebody, and from front of building to kitchen area; two levels then joined by 5/6 steps; stairs to first floor; every assistance will be given but all parts may not be accessible.
♿ & 🚻 welcome, phone in advance; contact Education staff to book an educational visit or take part in organised events. ◉

A treasure-house of 17th century objects, Bolling Hall is a superb building of the 15th to 18th centuries, furnished with appropriate period items, which you will find surrounded by domestic housing in the middle of modern Bradford. Few museums of this quality are in such an unlikely setting.

A tour of the hall begins on the ground floor of the late 14th or 15th century Pele Tower, the earliest part of the building. The Front Kitchen has a huge fireplace and all manner of 18th century cooking equipment. Above the fireplace is a clockwork mechanism formerly used to drive a spit, while a chimney crane and a Dutch oven show alternative methods of cooking by the heat of the flames. A vast oak meal-ark (or chest for storing food) of about 1600 dominates one wall, and a mid-17th century table sits under a stone-mullioned window. 17th century meat hooks, an oak spoon rack, and an 18th century oak cupboard are all typical kitchen objects of their periods. Bottles, brass pans, pewter and pottery add to the historic atmosphere.

The Back Kitchen has no fireplace, being the site of 'cold' processes such as dairying, equipment for which shown here includes butter churns and scales. Several types of mangle and a large 19th century box mangle, for

Exterior view of Bolling Hall

wringing out and pressing washing, reflect aspects of laundering, which also took place here. Under the stone floor of this room is a 17th Century rainwater cistern used to collect soft water for washing.

A small 'Study' contains 19th century diagonal barometers, and an earlier siphon barometer of about 1790. A brass water-clock on display is dated 1659, but is most probably a 19th century fake. There is also a terrestrial globe, of 1864; what changes the map of the world has seen since then!

A cabinet on a stand, dating from the mid-18th century, four walnut high-backed chairs of around 1685–90, and a longcase clock of about 1720 with a japanned case featuring an 'oriental' landscape, are some of the impressive items of furniture displayed in the panelled Parlour. But the most interesting piece, to my mind, is a life-sized dummy board. Such boards appeared in England for use as fire screens in the late 17th century, but later became purely ornamental. The one at Bolling portrays a lecherous oaf importuning an unfortunate woman.

The Housebody was the most important room in West Riding houses of the 16th and 17th centuries, and was a direct descendant of the medieval Hall. A number of items of 17th century furniture can be seen here, including oak chairs, an oak chest, table and benches, and a wonderful oak hall cupboard of 1628. Similar cupboards were often given as wedding presents in wealthy families. This room also has portraits of a woman and of a man by Michiel Jan Van Miereveld (1567–1644), a popular Dutch portraitist

whose style was formal, careful and orthodox. Livelier (if that's the word) is a rather disgruntled-looking boar's head. Arms and armour, and a series of heraldic stained-glass panels of about 1500 set into the window, add to the diversity of things to see in this airy room.

Beyond the Housebody is the later Georgian wing of the hall. Rooms here are furnished with 18th and early 19th century furniture. The Drawing Room contains a fine mahogany bookcase in the Chippendale 'Chinese' style, and a sofa with a gilt beech frame, both late 18th century. The Dining Room has chairs in Chippendale and Regency styles, and early 19th century dining

table, square piano in mahogany and satinwood, and beautiful sideboard. The dinner service displayed here is Derby porcelain of 1790–1800.

At the top of the staircase to the first floor hangs a portrait by Sir Joshua Reynolds of John, 2nd Earl of Egmont and his wife, Catherine. The Couch Room (or Red Bedroom) has a most opulent couch bed by Thomas Chippendale, the great Yorkshire furniture-maker. It was made for Harewood House, near Leeds, and is the only couch bed known to have survived from Chippendale's commissions. Nearby, there is an Edwardian bedroom, furnished with a bedroom suite of 1900–10.

Displays on the first floor of the 17th century East Tower feature some Civil War armour – boots, helmets, breast-plate and backplate, and swords – and cannonballs from the field of the battle of Adwalton Moor, fought in 1643 just before the 'seige' of Bradford. In an adjacent room are photographs and collections relating to the 16th/18th and 20th battalions of the West Yorkshire Regiment, the 'Bradford Pals', who volunteered in 1914/15 and were savaged at the Battle of the Somme on 1st July 1916.

The Ghost Room, Bolling Hall

Three more oak-panelled rooms on the first floor of the West wing have further very good examples of solid 17th century oak furniture. The Blue Room boasts a lovely inlaid oak chest of drawers, several 'Lancashire' type chairs, a tester bed of 1600–10 with floral inlay on the headboard, and an oak box with a sloping lid, probably used as a desk, carrying the initials IB. By the bed is a pewter chamber pot. Above the fireplace hangs a painting of a 17th century house. An adjacent room contains an 18th century lantern clock, and an intriguing 17th century cedar chest with 'pokerwork' inscribed design of fantastic creatures. Cedar was often used for chests as it was believed to give protection to the contents against moths.

The Horton Hall Room has a magnificent, richly decorated tester bed from Horton Old Hall of about 1600. A churchwarden's chest here of about 1500 is one of the earliest pieces of furniture in the house. Adorning one wall is a 17th century painting of 'A Sybil' by Francesco Del Cairo, a portrait study in light and shadow. A latrine built into the corner of this room reminds us that we are back in the medieval Pele Tower.

The Ghost Room has a carved oak overmantle and frieze, with elaborate plaster ceiling. Traditionally, this room was occupied by the Royalist Earl of Newcastle in 1643 during the Civil War, when a ghost appeared and entreated him to 'Pity Poor Bradford' and not, as he had ordered, to have the inhabitants massacred. A likely story! It first appeared in print in 1776.

In addition to the furniture collections of the highest quality, there is more to see in this fascinating old house. A room at the top of the Pele Tower has toys, dolls, a dolls' house and furniture, and children's furniture. Earlier items among the latter are a child's tiny oak chair of the early 17th century and a cradle of the late 17th/ early 18th century. A scrapwork screen dates from around 1870, and a toy washing machine, sink unit and cooker are of the 1960s, helping bring us back to more modern times.

Cartwright Hall

Lister Park, Bradford, West Yorkshire
BD9 4NS   (0274) 493313
Open daily. ▣ ▣
♿ W: all parts accessible, but access at rear of building and easier by prior arrangement with staff; disabled parking at rear of building.
⚥ & ⚥ welcome, phone in advance; contact Educational staff to book an educational visit or take part in organised events. ☺

Controversial local hero David Hockney is well represented among the collections of Cartwright Hall, the art gallery in the large park situated in the heart of industrial Bradford. Renowned for its lively exhibitions and performance art, Cartwright Hall is also particularly rich in Victorian paintings and sculpture.

Among earlier works in the gallery is one of the most famous of Cartwright Hall's paintings, the portrait of Master Thomas Lister (known as 'The Brown Boy') by Sir Joshua Reynolds. The leading portraitist of the 18th century is seen here at his finest. Young Thomas Lister, in relaxed yet grand pose, is set in an imaginary idyllic landscape. He wears a brown silk suit styled on 17th century clothes, with lace cuffs and collar, and slashed sleeves. Such dress was thought by Reynolds to be more timeless than contemporary clothes, which he considered looked ugly for portraits and would soon date them. But despite the care he took, Reynolds's portraits are firmly set in the 18th century, just as, for example, Sir John Lavery's 'Lady in a Green Coat' (*c.* 1903) is very definitely of the Edwardian era, likewise an age of elegance and poise. Lavery brings out the rich red hair of his model through contrast with her green coat.

The theme of children can be followed through other paintings at Cartwright Hall. 'The Princess and the Frog' by W.R. Symonds portrays the fairy tale in which a prince has been turned into a frog and must be kissed to become human again. 'The Pool' by

Reynolds, Thomas Lister, *1764(?)*

Symonds's contemporary, Edward Hornel, is interesting to compare in its thickly dabbed brushstrokes with the minutely-finished late 19th century picture by James Lobley, 'Little Nell Leaving the Church', inspired by Dickens's novel, *The Old Curiosity Shop.*

Carefully rendered detail is particularly characteristic of Victorian paintings, whether on contemporary themes or historical ones. The Victorians loved pictures that told stories, and historical narratives, like Wynford Dewhurst's 'An Ancient Stronghold in France', were especial favourites. The artists who made up the Pre-Raphaelite Brotherhood, and their many followers, made a great point of painting in minute detail, as well as using clear bright colours, often laid on a white ground, to convey light in their works. Ford Madox Brown's 'John Wycliffe Reading his Translation of the Bible to John of Gaunt' shows these characteristics, and also the stiffer poses and the type of dress that the artists admired in late medieval Italian paintings, from

Bertram Priestman, The Heart of the West Riding, *1916*

which they derived the name of their group (literally admirers of works pre-dating Raphael).

Other narrative paintings from the 19th and early 20th centuries at Cartwright Hall draw inspiration from Greek mythology. Wright Barker's 'Circe' is taken from Homer's *Odyssey*, and shows the enchantress that the hero, Ulysses, encountered on his way home from the Trojan War. Circe, surrounded by lions and wolves, and with red flowers strewn before her, provides a tempting welcome for the war-weary heroes. 'The Golden Fleece' by Herbert James Draper takes its story from the Greek tale of Jason and the Argonauts.

Recreations of ancient history were often an excuse for the depiction of nude and semi-clad figures, especially women. Edwin Long's 'An Egyptian Feast' has a multitude of figures, including dancing girls and musicians, watching a mummy being brought into the feast on a sledge (?!). Ernest Normand's 'The Bitter Draught of Slavery' is rather more sinister: a cowering white woman is being revealed before a thoughtful Arab by a black slave-trader, a second woman leaning desolate against a pillar, awaiting her turn. The whole thing reeks of sex and domination.

Seascapes and landscapes contrast with all the flesh. 'Old Folkestone' by James Webb and 'Off the Coast of Leghorn' by E.W. Cooke are two 19th century salty maritime pictures. A

J. C. Horsley, Pay for Peeping, *1872*

H. H. La Thangue, A Provençal Spring, *exhibited 1903*

larger-scale maritime work is Charles Joseph Staniland's 'The Emigrant Ship', in which it is the people who dominate the painting rather than the sea, thronging the quayside and ship, sorrowful and anxious at the prospect of the journey or the departure of loved ones. Bertram Priestman's 'The Heart of the West Riding' is a classic study of the local industrial townscape.

Bertram Priestman was born in Bradford, and local connections form another important thread at Cartwright Hall. David Hockney is the most famous of Bradford-born artists, and the collection incudes 'Le Plongeur', a colourful and dreamlike work featuring one of his favourite subjects, a swimming pool (colour plate 6). Yorkshire connections are likewise strong in the works of the sculptur, Henry Moore, whose drawings are also noteworthy and included in Cartwright Hall's collections.

William Rothenstein was the Bradford-born son of Jewish immigrants, and his painting 'The Browning Readers' is here; the artist's wife and sister-in-law posed for the work. Another striking picture of the early 20th century is 'The End of the Chapter' by Philip Wilson Steer. It shows a woman warming her hands by the fire in an elegant drawing room, her book resting on a chair. This painting offers an interesting contrast to some of Steer's more impressionist works, to be seen in other galleries in the North East.

Sculptures in a variety of materials and styles can also be found on display. There are both religious and secular pieces. Among the former, eleven carved and gilded marble reliefs, designed by the architect G.F. Bodley and carved by Farmer and Brindlay, are of note; they originally formed part of the reredos at St Paul's Cathedral in London, and depict angels carrying the instruments of the Passion of Christ (such as crown of thorns, scourge, nails, hammer, sponge, and dice). George Frampton's bronze 'Madonna of the Peach Tree' is also striking. A 19th century life-size marble by Giovanni Battista Lombardi takes for its subject the biblical Susanna,

Ernest Sichel, The Necklace

National Museum of Photography, Film and Television

Prince's View, Bradford, West Yorkshire BD5 OTR   (0274) 727488
Closed Mondays. ▣ (but ⬧ for IMAX auditorium)
▣ ♿W
⚺ & ⚹ must book in advance. ☉

When Joseph Nicéphore Niépce finally managed to fix a permanent photographic image onto a pewter plate some time before 1826, he cannot have imagined how the world 150 years later would have come to take the photograph completely for granted. This museum explains how photography has developed and how it has affected our lives and the way we see ourselves. Television and film, media that are allied to photography, are also explained.

Photography had no beginning as such, unless it be the realisation in 5th century BC China that light could be focused through a hole onto a surface. Serious attempts to capture an image

created by light in a camera (originally *camera obscura* or 'dark room') were first made in the late 18th century by Thomas Wedgwood, son of the famous Josiah the potter. It was Niépce who actually managed it, and the museum's reproduction of the view from his window at Gras in France in 1826 is evidence of one of the most momentous of all scientific discoveries.

In its various galleries the museum's displays describe the way photographic images are created, and there are plenty of opportunities for visitors to try their hand at so doing, using the panoramic views of Bradford city centre from the building's large glass bow front. There are not, in the main body of the museum, many real historical objects or photographs. Instead the emphasis is very much on the science of the creation of images and the demonstration of technique, and the use of descriptive graphics.

Among the real things on display are daguerreotypes by Antoine Claudet, one of the most celebrated of daguerreotype makers. The process was discovered by and named after Louis Daguerre, a Frenchman like Niépce, whose images were produced on plates of copper coated with silver. These

observed at her bath by some elders – a subject more usually seen in old master paintings. Smaller secular pieces include 'The Kiss', a delightful marble relief by Arthur G. Walker, and four delicate bronzes by Ernest Sichel. 'Humanity Overcoming War' by F. Derwent Wood is a large and dramatic allegorical marble sculpture, with the female Humanity vanquishing a strong creature that has the head of a man but the breasts of a woman.

Food for thought, certainly, as well as visual enjoyment, among the art collections at this most Yorkshire of galleries.

Jabez Hogg photographing Mr Johnson, c.1843 – the first known photo of a photographer at work

A display in the Kodak Museum

images were of a brilliant clarity, but each was unique and could not be reproduced. Ultimately it proved to be a dead-end in the development of photography, but daguerreotypes remain the most magical of all photographic images.

The displays show how the other very early photographic process, the calotype, provided the way forward to the albumen and wet collodion processes, and eventually the gelatin-based process we know today. There are (modern) prints of photographs taken by the Scottish masters, David Hill and Robert Adamson and the English inventor of the calotype process, William Henry Fox Talbot. Cartes-de-visite and ferrotypes illustrate the popularisation of the photographic image, joined in a section on portrait photography by the morbid images of dead children common in an age of high infant mortality.

An atmospheric reproduction of a 1932 photographic studio contains Sichel's giant 'Forward' Studio Camera, with striking portraits by Paul Tanqueray of the actresses Gertrude Lawrence and Tallulah Bankhead.

To my mind, the most interesting (and least technical) section on photography is the one dealing with News Photography. Here the power of the camera really comes to life. At one point the impact of the news photo-

The Kodak 'No. 1' camera

graph is compared with film: so we have studies of Jack Ruby's shooting of Lee Harvey Oswald in 1963, the storming of the Iranian Embassy by the SAS in 1980, the return of British troops from the Falklands in 1982, mounted police charging pickets at Orgreave Coking Works in 1984. The way a camera can lie is another effective exhibit, with that masterful study by American Civil War photographer, Alexander Gardner, of the 'Home of a Rebel Sharpshooter' at Gettysburg in 1893, revealed to be largely fiction, the only truth being the dead soldier whose body Gardner moved and posed.

The News Photography section has other memorable images: the haunting eyes of Moors Murderess Myra Hindley; the explosion of HMS Antelope in the Falkands War (captioned as 'blaze

of glory' by the *Daily Mail*; 'senseless sacrifice' by the *Morning Star*); Leon Trotsky speechmaking, captured on film by Robert Capa; and a marvellous study of Arthur Scargill, armed with a megaphone and wearing a baseball cap, confronting the massed ranks of riot police in Orgreave. A lighter side of the miners' strike of 1984–85 is shown by the photograph of a policeman in conversation with a miner wearing a toy policeman's helmet.

The Kodak Museum is housed within the NMPFT. It contains lots of photographic images and the entire spectrum of cameras large and small, expensive and cheap, successful and not so successful.

The NMPFT always has a number of temporary exhibitions of photographs on view. On my visit the best showed works by Karsh, whose portraits of Peter Lorre, Nikita Khrushchev, Humphrey Bogart and Boris Karloff are among the most unforgettable of modern images; and by Julia Margaret Cameron, the Victorian portraitist, one of whose albums of photographs is owned by the museum.

The television galleries are most popular with the technically-minded, also with those who like pushing lots of buttons or otherwise participating in a museum display. Most dramatic is the 'Beauty and the Beast' stage set, with an opportunity to operate TV cameras. Causing most hilarity is the chance to read the news and then see yourself on a TV screen – I have never seen museum visitors laugh so much! All too brief are snatches of TV programmes from the past – Billy Bunter, 'Z' Cars', Robin Hood, 'The Saint', the 1966 World Cup, 'Steptoe and Son', Yosser Hughes in 'The Boys from the Blackstuff'. There are some historic television sets and bits of insides of the same, but in these galleries it is the moving image that hypnotises.

A special feature of NMPFT is its IMAX cinema, with 'Britain's biggest cinema screen'. Films are shown during the day and on some evenings. The films shown during the day are specially made for the huge IMAX projector and screen, and are well worth a visit if you can stand heights.

DONCASTER

The Museum of South Yorkshire Life

Cusworth Hall, Cusworth Lane, Doncaster, South Yorkshire DN5 7TU
(0302) 782342
Closed Fridays. F P
& S: main entrance has flight of steps – assistance to lift wheelchairs given whenever possible, advance notice preferred (lift allowing access to ground floor soon to be installed); no further steps on ground floor; stairs only to first floor.
& book in advance: contact Curator or secretary.
wishing to use special educational facilities in Study Centre contact Education Officer (0302) 786925 a year in advance, although general visits can sometimes be accommodated at short notice; evenings by special arrangement. ☺

This 1740s country house is not all that it first appears. Instead of the expected endless succession of period rooms with Chippendale-style chairs, Sheraton-style tables and Adam-style fireplaces, Cusworth Hall houses a sizable and popular social history museum of great variety and interest, which is well worth a visit. All human life is here, from birth to death, with most things in between (including bed-bugs!), much of it with intelligent commentary.

Both women and men at work are featured. Displays observe the changing role of women in Victorian England and up to the First World War, but point out that working-class women did not need to clamour for 'real' work, in that they had long worked in mines, factories and urban sweatshops.

The most memorable displays on men at work concern coalmining, in a section entitled 'Black Diamonds'. This contains the obligatory ceremonial spade and wheelbarrow, but goes so far as to have some real coal on view as well, and a tin bath. Less nostalgic are the tragic souvenir serviettes of the Cadeby Colliery disaster of 1912, when after an initial explosion killed over thirty men, a second explosion entombed the rescuers. Mining communities have always been haunted by the fear of accident, illness and death. An astonishing statistic is that during 1922–24 over half a million miners were injured at work (this excludes anyone who stayed away from work for less than one week). In 1926 850 miners were injured *every day*, five were maimed every ten minutes, and one was killed every five hours. It is in the light of such risks that we should see the miners' 1926 General Strike slogan: 'Not a penny off the pay / Not a second on the day.'

Peering down on the reminders of this carnage, safe and framed above the marble fireplace, is a member of the Battie-Wrightson family, which owned Cusworth Hall between 1740 and 1952. The Battie-Wrightsons – splendid name! – crop up from time to time around the hall, as does the occasional piece of high quality oak furniture. Outstanding among these are a servant's chair of the 18th century, and a carved cupboard, although the furniture does tend to get overwhelmed by the sheer volume of more prosaic material. Difficult to overwhelm, nevertheless, is the monstrous oak Sprotbrough parish chest, early medieval in date and ten feet long, which is basically a hollowed-out tree.

Other types of local employment range from railways to farming and crafts. The displays tell us that while 'women's crafts' are regarded today as hobbies or pastimes, and are rarely taken seriously, in the past quilting, rag-rugmaking, sewing, lacemaking and spinning were essential parts of the local economy.

Children at work is an important theme in the Children's Room. Children who would be regarded today as too young to stay up after eight o'clock at night used to be employed in the mines, on farms, in brickmaking, grinding forks, tilemaking, glasswork-

The Sprotbrough parish chest

Thomas Rowlandson, Doncaster Fair or the Industrious Yorkshirebites

ing, glovemaking and domestic service, as well as up chimneys. Victorian values were not completely unattractive, and the nation that conquered, converted and exploited much of the world did give a few of its own children the chance to enjoy their childhood. Victorian and Edwardian toys have a mystical quality about them, and they always make bright displays. At Cusworth they are joined by later toys and games in a room likely to be packed with visitors.

Among the toys are some identified as being 'best', in other words the preserve of the wealthy. Here we find a Noah's Ark complete with cargo – a Sunday toy in those households where only toys with biblical connections were allowed on the Sabbath. There is a colourful set of Snap (Snip-snap-snorum) cards, including Hokey Pokey!, All Hot and Floury!, Old Clo!, and Cat's Meat! This section also has two lovely felt dolls from the 1920s.

More and more items evoke the magic of childhood, from a working train and tram layout (action for 10p), to home-made amusements (which survive much more rarely than expensive, shop-bought toys) such as clothes-peg dolls; and lead animals given away with cocoa in the 1930s, to street games. An extract from Winifred Renshaw's *An Ordinary Life* refers to children playing certain games at certain times of year: 'and I don't know how we knew when to start. One day there were no skipping ropes and the next every little girl would be twirling one.' Hoops, whipping tops, skipping ropes, hopscotch, battledore and shuttlecock are all here, with marbles, knucklebones and a newspaper kite. The children's theme is maintained in displays on education (dumb bells, exercise clubs, abacus), and on clothing, including a dinky pair of mock-snakeskin boy's boots.

Other general themes dealt with in various sections of this super museum include Entertainment, Costume, Wartime Life, and Transport.

'What did the Mouse say to Felix? Cheese It!': a cheese advert from Stubbs the grocers of Askern (closed 1929) is one of many lively and cheer-

Cheese advert from Stubbs the grocers of Askern

ful (and some not so cheerful) illustrations distributed all around Cusworth Hall. The New Acquisitions case when I visited had an Oxo painting book of the 1930s – *Percy Vere with Oxo* – and a picture of Gracie Fields adorning her own *Book of Words*.

You come across a variety of pictures. The painting 'Fairy Tales' by W.T.C. Dobson sentimentalises childhood; Ralph Wilford's 'Yorkshire Main Pit, Edlington', captures a pit closed in 1986; Thomas Rowlandson's 'Doncaster Fair or the Industrious Yorkshirebites' portrays a group of bucolic locals playing 'wallops' (sticks thrown at skittles, of course!). On her sampler of 1837 Henrietta Binns warns us: 'In early youth redeem your time / Not loose a moment in your prime / The time may come when you may mourn / The season lost which cant return.'

In addition to the enormous variety of permanent displays, many different subjects are dealt with in the museum's lively temporary exhibition programme. At the time I was there, you could find hundreds of postcards throughout the hall on a bewildering variety of subjects – travel, cats, Doncaster, nursing, European transporter bridges,

the Saints of Ireland, women's eyes, babies, French Christmas, grandad's pin-ups 1910–18. Two sets of particular note related to warfare. The first, 'Sketches of Tommy's Life' gave glimpses of life on the Western Front in 1914–18: 'The only time I ever saw a man cry / was when one of our chaps dropped / his rifle in the mud after spending / exactly two hours cleaning it.' The second series brought the nuclear debate into the museum. One postcard, entitled '147 False Alarms' showed a scene inside the Main Control Room: 'Whoops!! Sir we just wiped out Europe'.

Another temporary exhibition dealt with Health and Beauty. It was very reassuring, with all sorts of machines, mechanisms and medications to render the body beautiful. The trouble is that you only find these things in museums, never for sale anywhere. I'd love to have a go at Sir Hiram Maxim's Pipe of Peace and Maxim Inhaler, or the Punkt Roller (sixty suction caps to roll over the body to 'attack' the entire skin surface). I don't yet need the RE-DUCA Chin-Strap ('Away with Double Chin!') at 3s 6d from hairdressers (which ones?!) but there are lots of people who'd no doubt like one.

DURHAM

Durham Cathedral Treasury

Durham Cathedral, The College,
Durham DH1 3EH　(091) 386 2489
Open daily. 🅰🖼🅿　♿W
Enquiries: Treasury Custodian
(091) 384 4854

Durham Cathedral is one of the world's most stupendous buildings. It dates largely from the period 1093–1133, with later towers and chapels, and is the most complete surviving Anglo-Norman church. It is also the burial place of St Cuthbert, Bishop of Lindisfarne 685–687 AD, and the North's greatest saint. Relics of Cuthbert, with other ancient and beautiful objects associated with the Cathedral, can be seen in the Treasury Museum.

Cuthbert was originally buried on Lindisfarne where he died. However, in order to secure his body from Viking raids in the 9th century, monks took it from the island and wandered over the North of England until settling at Durham in 995. The body, still in a good state of preservation, was enshrined behind the High Altar at Durham in 1104, and for over 400 years pilgrims flocked to the city. The shrine was thrown down at the Reformation and Cuthbert's body was simply buried on the spot. In 1827 the grave was opened to reveal a series of three coffins, the innermost containing a skeleton swathed in silk. The earliest of the coffins and several artefacts were removed and the bones were reburied.

The remains of St Cuthbert's coffin and those artefacts are in the Treasury. The coffin is oak, and bears incised figures of Christ, the four Evangelists, the Twelve Apostles, the Seven Archangels, the Virgin and the Child and other symbols. Three of the items from the coffin are believed to be personal belongings of Cuthbert – a portable altar, a pectoral cross and (rather less likely to have been his) an ivory comb. The altar is only about five inches square, made of oak encased in silver plates bound with silver straps. The silver is a later enshrinement, possibly of the 8th century. The cross is gold inset with garnets, dated around 640–670, and is possibly Northumbrian.

On his visit to Cuthbert's shrine in 934, then in Chester-le-Street, King Aethelstan presented to the shrine a stole, maniple and girdle, now also displayed in the Treasury. They are of gold threads and coloured silks on silk foundations, depicting Old Testament Prophets, a Pope and attendant deacons, and foliage designs. Both stole and maniple were made at the command of Queen Aelfflaed (died 916). In addition there are three more fragments of braids of the same period. These items are fabulous examples of Anglo-Saxon religious art.

Of about the same age as Cuthbert's coffin is an illustrated *Commentary on the Psalms* by Cassiodorus Senator, one of a collection of books and manuscripts in the Treasury. The *Commentary* is Northumbrian with richly decorated frontispieces painted in vermillion, green, yellow and purple. It may have come from Bede's monastery of St Paul at **Jarrow**.

An illustrated Bible of about 1083–96 features Prophets and Evangelists, foliage and the heads of beasts in browns, reds, greens, blues and pur-

Parts of stole and maniple

Virgin & Child enthroned, St Cuthbert's coffin

ples. An illuminated bible of about 1170–80 has even more elaborate decoration with great care taken over the detailing of faces and clothing of figures.

Other early items are three gold rings with sapphires of the late 11th to mid-12th century from the graves of Bishops Flambard, Rufus and Ste Barbe. Another, later ring of the 16th century was found in the tomb of Bede. Also 11th century are a pair of sandals and fragments of silk cloth with silver gilt thread, from the grave of Bishop St Calais. The head of a bishop's crozier of iron covered with silver sheets comes from an unidentified grave, but is datable to about 1066–1140 from its animal interlace pattern. A lead funerary chalice of the early 12th century came from the grave of Bishop Flambard, and a second lead chalice possibly came from the monastic cemetary.

The most intriguing of the other medieval items is undoubtedly the great 12th century Sanctuary Knocker from the north door of the Cathedral. Like other places the Cathedral had the right of sanctuary throughout the Middle Ages, and criminals arriving at the north door to claim protection had

Sanctuary knocker, Durham Cathedral

to summon the watchman by using the knocker. The protection of the Church was thus extended, and the criminal's choice was between trial and exile.

The Conyers Falchion is a 13th century sword, almost one metre long, with curved steel blade, bronze guard and pommel with a wooden grip. The guard is decorated with winged biting serpents, the pommel bears a black eagle and the Arms of England. The sword was presented to the Bishop by the Conyers family as a symbolic military service in return for the Manor of Stockburn. Embroidered copes, alabaster sculptures and the sumptuous Auckland Castle Plate can all be seen in the Treasury, together with seals, books, accounts and other Cathedral relics and records.

You should also visit the Cathedral, itself a wonder of the medieval world, which contains many more items of interest. The tombs of Bede and St Cuthbert are here, as is the front of 'Father Smith's Great Organ', a late 17th century monster. Even more impressive is Prior Castell's huge clock of the early 16th century.

Just across Palace Green from the Cathedral is Durham Castle, another mighty edifice atop the city's rocky peninsula. Guided tours around the

Castle (to which there is an admission charge) give access to this majestic building and to its collections. The best parts of the building interior are the Tudor buttery and kitchen, the Great Hall, the Black Staircase, the Norman doorway in Tunstal's Gallery, Tunstal's Chapel, the Norman Gallery and the Norman Chapel with its original herringbone stone floor.

The 13th and 14th century Great Hall contains military relics from the Napoleonic period, and an extraordinary set of twenty-eight small 17th century breastplates and helmets said to have been for boys conscripted in the Civil War period.

Auckland Castle alms dish

Tunstal's Gallery houses a massive 700-year-old oak chest, too tempting for 14th century thieves who had their hands chopped off for trying to break into it. Further along the Gallery is a set of 17th century saddles in excellent condition with cavalry pistol holders, basket-hilted swords and muskets, all towered over by a magnificent Norman doorway, one of the best examples of Norman stone carving in the country. Nearby is a terracotta bust of George II by the famous sculptor John Michael Rysbrack (1694–1770), 18th century militia drums, 19th century weapons and Wedgwood pottery

Together, Durham Cathedral and its Treasury and Durham Castle make for the most unusual of visits in the most spectacular surroundings.

The Oriental Museum

University of Durham, Elvet Hill, Durham DH1 3TH   (091) 374 2911
Closed Saturdays and Sundays November to February. 🏢 🅿
♿ S: wheelchair access to Egyptian Gallery, Writing Room and Chinese bed only.
🚻 & 👥 contact Museum Secretary; small discount for groups booked at least a week in advance.

This is the home of a glorious collection of Eastern art – Chinese, Japanese, Indian, Burmese, Thai – with Egyptian and other Near and Middle-Eastern material. The variety of fantastic shapes and brilliant colours, and the powerful imagery of these great civilisations, is quite stunning.

The museum has treasures in abundance, but the Chinese pottery and porcelain dominate, ranging from 2–3,000 BC up to the present century. The early, more primitive ceramics are earthenware with distinctive shapes and decorations, for example a dark grey pottery *li*, a tripod cooking vessel with a short body and three short legs of about 1500–1000 BC. The inventiveness of Chinese potters, which was to reach such heights in later centuries, was already evident in Han dynasty pottery (206 BC to 220 AD), like the remarkable glazed pottery model here of a farmyard complete with reposing pig!

The T'ang dynasty (618–906 AD) saw the production of many types of ceramics for every conceivable use – bowls, vases, dishes, plates, as well as religious and other figures. Of especial note among the earthenware from this period are two Bactrian camels from North China, and a marvellous tomb figure of a woman dressed as a man, on horseback playing polo. This may be a model of Yang Gue-gei, a favourite imperial courtesan who is reputed to have played polo, normally a man's game. The T'ang period also witnessed the production of the world's first porcelains, with their vitrified, translu-

T'ang dynasty camel

cent bodies. The classic age of Chinese ceramics was the Sung period (960–1279), and the museum has large numbers of wares, including Chün stoneware and Lung-ch'üan celadon wares.

The Yüan period (1280–1368) saw even greater innovation, blue and white porcelain being made for the first time.

The Ming dynasty (1368–1644) is noted for a vast scale of production of very beautiful porcelain, both blue and white, and polychrome, decorated with trees, flowers, birds, dragons, fish and human figures. All decorations were symbolic. The lotus was associated with Buddhism, for which the flower was a sign of perfection, a symbol of purity among the evil of the world. For the Chinese the lotus also represented fertility, prosperity, peace and tranquility. The bamboo represented vigour, durability and integrity, the peony good fortune, the chrysanthemum longevity.

The Ch'ing dynasty (1644–1912) produced ceramics of exceptional quality, including the polychrome wares known as *famille verte* and *famille rose*. The beauty of the best of these, as displayed in the Oriental Museum, is unsurpassed anywhere in the world.

Chinese artistry is represented in other materials in the museum, notably in stone and bronze. Many animals are featured, such as a carved stone tomb figure of the Chinese zodiac hare from the Sui period (581–618 AD), Yüan

Japanese lacquer cabinet, 1860–80

bronze horses, and a Ming bronze water buffalo and a lion. Other bronze animals were produced as personal adornment in the Ordos region from the 5th century BC to the 5th century AD, in a style common to nomadic races of Eurasia.

Jade and lacquer are two more materials worked in by the Chinese. The Hardinge Collection of jades at the museum is enormous, from axes and knife blades to *Gui*, symbols of authority, and *Bi*, disc symbols of heaven; and to amulets, pendants, belt hooks and buckles, personal ornaments, and even musical instruments. Because it is harder than steel, carving jade took titanic effort and skill, which explains why it was so highly valued. The museum has many more hard-stone carvings in addition to the jades.

Lacquerwork usually consists of a wooden base with layers of lacquer from the sap of trees built up on it and decorated. The Chinese excelled in this art form, and among the splendid collection of Chinese and Japanese lacquerwork is an extravagant red lacquer box of 1736–95, decorated with signs for spring, good luck and longevity (ill. on cover). Another striking lacquer piece is a deep red Ming dish, decorated with a dragon, symbol of the emperor, and a phoenix, symbol of the empress.

Yang Gue-gei(?) playing polo, T'ang dynasty

Other items of sparkling quality include examples of Chinese costume, especially a dragon robe with elaborate embroidery representing bats (happiness and longevity), swastikas (abundance, Buddha's heart), clouds (beneficial rain), and many more motifs; snuff boxes; a T'ang cast-iron horse; and a huge bed.

A lacquer cabinet, fans, carvings, writing boxes, arms and kites form the nucleus of the Japanese collections. The museum has a lively collection of *netsuke* – small toggles to fasten items to the traditional sashes worn by Japanese men and women, such as seal boxes or medicine boxes known as *inro*. *Netsuke* were made of lacquered wood or bamboo, ivory and other materials, and were carved in almost an infinity of shapes.

Other cultures in South-East Asia are represented by further dazzling sculptures, carvings and paintings. A

Ancient Egyptian serving girl figure

Royal Palace balcony in Burma provided a series of carved teak panels of about 1700, of wonderful quality. More modern, but just as compelling, are a Shiva figure from India, dancing to the rhythm of the cosmic order, and a Balinese carving of a Ramayana epic scene, wherein Sita is kidnapped and threatened by Ravena holding a dagger in his hand, and is rescued by Jatayu, the mythological bird of protective power.

The Egyptian collection was begun in the 1820s by the Duke of Northumberland. It was eventually purchased by Durham University, and has since been added to. It is a fine example of a 19th century private collection, with many choice items including some excellent *shabtis* and an extensive range of amulets.

Shabtis were originally the images of the deceased buried along with the corpse so as to act as a substitute for the dead person in the compulsory labour of the next world. Eventually,

corpses were buried with many *shabtis*, who were to act as slaves. These figures were made of fine stones and woods, faience and other materials. Tiny figures of gods and goddesses were carried about by Egyptians as amulets. They come in all the mystical shapes of the gods, and the museum has Ptah, Amun, Min, Horus, Nefertem, Shu, Maat, Mut, Thoth, Selket, Osiris, Isis and many more.

Other notable Egyptian items include a carved boxwood figure of a servant girl of the 18th Dynasty (1580–1314 BC), the mummy of a boy aged about eight years, the mummy and coffin of a one-handed priest (his missing hand was represented by one made of linen), and a red granite obelisk of Amenophis II (*c.* 1450–1425 BC). This last was dedicated to the god Khnum, and was discovered in use as a threshold in a house in Aswan.

Examples of early forms of writing – Mesopotamian, Egyptian, Chinese and others – are to be seen at the museum, reinforcing the sense of high civilisation that the rest of the collections convey. The Oriental Museum is a shrine to oriental beliefs and the finest in oriental decorative arts, to which many more people should make a pilgrimage.

Balinese carving of a Ramayana scene

Cat of Bastet

GATESHEAD

Shipley Art Gallery

Prince Consort Road, Gateshead,
Tyne and Wear NE8 4JB
(091) 477 1495
Closed Mondays. **F**
♿: steps at entrance (attendants on hand to assist), but otherwise all on one level.
👥 & 👤 welcome, book in advance if talk or tour required; small groups can visit stores by prior arrangement.

The heart of the Shipley Art Gallery's collections are the paintings bequeathed to the borough of Gateshead by Joseph Shipley in 1909. At the time, his private collection was the subject of mixed views, and in fact the city of Newcastle refused Shipley's bequest before Gateshead accepted it. Even sixty years later, the Shipley's collection was not well known, nor fashionable. Today, it stands as a delightful provincial collection with some outstanding works.

The British paintings have no masterpieces among them, but there are some interesting paintings of different styles and periods. Among the earlier works is 'Eight Years Old' (1632) by Gilbert Jackson, a charming study of a little girl and her dog. Somewhat later, but looking rather more 17th than 19th century, is 'The Sons of Thomas Dallas' by George Watson (1769–1837).

Of the mid-19th century paintings, William James Grant's 'Juliet and the Friar, "Take Thou This Phial"' is painted in a painstakingly detailed style reminiscent of the Pre-Raphaelites. Two works by the popular Atkinson Grimshaw are quite different from one another. The leafy 'November Morning, Knostrop Hall, Leeds, 1883', shows the exterior of the house where he lived for a time, while the moonlit, grey-green, silhouetted 'Greenwich, Half Tide, 1884' is more typical of the works for which Grimshaw is best known. Frederick Mason Sheard's

Frederick Mason Sheard, Harvesters Resting, *1898*

'Harvesters Resting' (1898) glows with colour, while John Arthur Dees's 'The Dog Daisy Field, Low Fell, 1910' is clearly Edwardian, with gambolling children. Among the watercolours are a meticulous work by the Pre-Raphaelite, William Henry Hunt, 'Still Life With Fruit', and one by the bird painter, Charles Frederick Tunnicliffe, 'The Ninth Wave' (*c.* 1949), with cartoon-effect seagulls and waves.

However, it is the Dutch and Flemish works – and a single great Venetian painting – that comprise the best of the Shipley's collections. Most of these were acquired by Joseph Shipley, who seems to have chosen paintings that pleased him, and at moderate prices, rather than by well-known masters. As taste turns circle again, Shipley's own choice is far more fashionable now than it was in his lifetime.

Jacob Grimmer's 'Landscape with Scenes from the Story of Tobias and The Angel' is one of the earlier paintings, and is the only work by him in a British public collection. It was probably painted in the 1570s, and is a combination of figures in a landscape that varies from sombre greenery to warm pink buildings. Pieter Balten's

Janssens,
Diana and her Companions

'St John the Baptist Preaching' (1590s) is altogether a much busier painting, of a crowd listening to St John, based upon a painting by Pieter Breughel the Elder. Balten's work is colourful, the figures are bold, and there is a naive quality about the whole. The detail –

Roubiliac, Alexander Pope, *1741*

Hall cabinet/sideboard by Fred Baier, 1983

Alison Britton, Teaspot, *1980*

birds in baskets, hunting dogs, musical instruments, and the costume of men, women and children – is tremendous.

'The Temptation of Adam and Eve' (1614) by Joachim Anthonisz. Wttewael is one of the Shipley's exceptional paintings, an example of Dutch mannerism. Of about the same date is another important work, 'Diana and Her Companions' by Abraham Janssens, showing a group with the huntress Diana, and still lifes of the animals, captured in the great Flemish tradition. Dirck van Delen's 'Game of Skittles' from around the 1630s is an imaginary architectural scene, with figures possibly added by another artist, Anthony Palamedes. This is a lovely painting, with great clarity in the foreground, and increasingly ghostly figures in the background.

David Teniers the Younger's 'Tavern Scene' (*c.* 1640s) is a scene of everyday low-life, painted in minute detail. Adriaen Pietersz. van de Venne's 'Peasants Brawling' is another low-life scene of beggars fighting, captioned 'it is pitiful' by the artist. Van de Venne's paintings are typically very revealing about the real poor, which in itself makes him fairly unusual.

The Venetian work of note is 'Christ Washing the Disciples' Feet' (1547) by Jacopo Tintoretto. It is huge in scale, with glittering light, and dramatic movement of figures. Tintoretto was a great master who had an influence on many artists, both contemporary and later. Italian Old Master works of such quality are rare in the North East, so Gateshead should be on every art lover's itinerary for this painting alone!

Apart from paintings, the Shipley has some very fine items of furniture, glass and silver, and some sculptures. Pride of place among the latter goes to Louis François Roubiliac's bust of the poet and satirist, Alexander Pope (1741). Roubiliac was the most talented sculptor working in England in the mid-18th century, and this bust, which may once have been owned by David Garrick, the actor, is typical of his vivid realism.

The most flamboyant piece of furniture is the Shakespeare Sideboard (*c.* 1860) by Gerrard Robinson, a leading wood carver, who was born and worked in Newcastle. He specialised in detailed naturalistic carving, and this enormous sideboard is alive with scenes from Shakespeare, including the witches from *Macbeth,* the corpulent Falstaff, and Hamlet's reflections over Yorick's skull.

The glassmaking company of Sowerby & Co. of Gateshead were most renowned for their clear pressed glass, but they also produced attractive coloured blown glass. Both types can be seen at the Shipley in a dazzling array of colours – yellows, blues, black, white, greens, and clear glass – in an extraordinary variety of forms.

As well as for its Dutch and Flemish paintings, the Shipley is well known for its collections of contemporary crafts. These are a wonderland of fantastic colours and designs, ranging from jewellery to furniture. Every conceivable material is used in creating new shapes and styles, and the informal displays of crafts nicely complement the more formal arrangements of sculptures and paintings. Items that stood out on my visit were some dolls by Julia Hills, a laminated rocking horse, a hall cabinet in birch and sycamore with a tartan top (!), and the splendid Cat Car by Frank and Bridget Egerton. Crafts can be boring, but these are exhilarating!

Julia Hills, 'Grimaldi' doll, 1978

HALIFAX
Shibden Hall and Folk Museum

*Halifax, West Yorkshire HX3 6XG
(0422) 52246*
Closed December and January, and only open Sundays in February. 🔊 ▣ 🅿
♿ **S**: wheelchair access to ground-floor display areas; steps in barn and workshop areas, but these can be negotiated; no wheelchair access to first floor of house.
🚻 & 🚹 book in advance contact Lettings Section at Wellesley Park, Halifax (0422) 59454. ☼

History and tranquility are combined in Shibden Hall, the pride of Halifax, an ancient centre of the West Yorkshire woollen industry. A superlative yeoman's house set in the ninety-acre Shibden Park, the museum has extremely high quality collections of furniture, furnishings, craft tools, and items relating to rural life.

The hall itself dates back to the 15th century. The focal point of the kitchen is the stone fireplace, occupied by an iron cauldron and basket spit, and surrounded by earthenware bottles and jars, salt box, warming pan and other implements. Pewter, copper, brass and ironwork complement the huge oak dresser of about 1700 and the stone-flagged floor. A tinder box, mahogany cheese boat, cheese kettle, game rack, coffee mill, sugar cutters, blunderbuss and mouse trap suggest a way of life that, while long gone, remains familiar in many ways.

A through passage, which leads to the Study, contains an 18th century settle, a longcase clock by Thomas Lister of Halifax, and an 18th century diagonal barometer. The pine-panelled Study is also furnished in 18th century manner, with Hepplewhite-style chairs, bureau and card table. On the bureau are brass candlesticks, a clay pipe, a sander and quills. Drinking glasses and a toddy

The Study, Shibden Hall

bowl indicate gentlemanly pleasures other than reading and writing. A kestrel wearing a splendid hood points to livelier pursuits. Hawking has a long history and was a widespread pastime of the gentry in the 17th century. The sporting guns in the study ushered in a new age of hunting.

The main living room of the house, known as the Housebody, has some good quality furniture, although it is the superb stained glass windows that catch the eye, particularly when the sunshine streams through them into the room. A late 16th century oak table, a Thomas Deykinm longcase clock with elaborate marquetry, a court cupboard, 17th century armour and a tiny 17th century stumpwork panel are some of the best items here.

The Tudor Savile Room is presented as an 18th century ladies' withdrawing room, with cello, flute, piano, embroidery, tea caddy, brass kettle, ceramics and glass, and a mixture of Hepplewhite-style and Chippendale-style chairs. More musical instruments are next door in the Dining Room, which also contains a lovely fireplace, and a brass bracket clock with a frantic tick!

The high quality continues on the first floor. In the Oak Room are wigs,

The Housebody, looking towards the stained glass windows

16th century maiolica drug jar

Tudor chairs of 1579. A Victorian Nursery (with see-saw) and an Edwardian bedroom complete the upper floor displays.

A range of farm buildings behind Shibden Hall house important collections relating to the rural area around Halifax, and interesting items of transport. The transport is displayed in a proud 17th century barn. The most elegant vehicle is the Lister Chaise of the early 18th century, almost matched by a state chariot of the late 18th century and a Landau of the late 19th

Leeds pottery, a prayer niche and an unusual 19th century longcase clock by S. S. Pinchin. The North Chamber boasts eighteen-inch-wide oak floorboards; the Powder Closet contains more wigs, a shoehorn, bellows, and 18th century slippers; and the Tower Landing has a stag's head chair. A tremendous bed of about 1630 inhabits the Red Room; the yellow livery of the 5th Earl of Londsdale is kept in the livery cupboard in the Porch Chamber Passage, which has 15th century floorboards. The Porch Chamber contains some very early furniture, notably some

View of the farm buildings

century. A drag, a Gypsy vardo and a sedan chair were different modes of travel for the healthy, a 1912 ambulance was for the sick, and an ornate but sinister hearse for the dead. Nearby is an extensive collection of harness, a gigantic pair of boots and, in winter, a roaring fire to keep the circulation going.

Other farm buildings contain a dairy, with churns, troughs, yokes, cheese vats and a cheese press, and a brewhouse, with its own vats and troughs. Implements include a wooden plough, hay turner, scythe, threshing machine, mill, harrow, seed drill and two flat wagons. An ancient sheep salving bench and sheep shears are reminders of the importance of sheep farming in the region. Outside a horse wheel is a relic of the days when animals were the main source of power on the farm.

Hearse, Shibden Hall

A series of craft workshops, an apothecary's, a pub and a cottage are arranged around a courtyard. All contain notable collections. The pub has a pair of fighting cocks doing each other mischief in a showcase. The weaver's cottage is a particularly successful reconstruction, with its pots, bowls, spades and cradle. The cooper's, wheelwright's and blacksmith's are replete with the tools of their trades and their products.

Shibden has about it a timeless quality that gives an impression of past society, which is rarely equalled in the region. It is a gem of a museum, with collections to match its architectural splendour.

HULL

Ferens Art Gallery

Queen Victoria Square, Hull, North Humberside HU1 3RA
(0482) 222750
Open daily. 🄵 ▣
♿ **S**: wheelchair access to ground floor only.
🍴 & 👥 advance booking preferred: contact Curator. ◷

Famed for its maritime paintings, the Ferens Art Gallery has the most complete collection of Dutch Old Master works, and the most impressive series of portraits, for many a mile. Among these is arguably the most important painting in the entire region, a masterpiece by a sublime genius.

Hull's greatness was based on the sea, and it is fitting that one of the most extensive collections of maritime paintings in the country is in the city that gave birth to its own school of marine artists in the 19th century. Of this school 'The Return of the "William Lee"' by John Ward is the peak of achievement, showing the former whaling ship entering Humber Dock

basin in full sail after a voyage to Calcutta. The 'William Lee' was lost in 1847. 'Hull from Paull' is a fine work by William Barton. One of Ward's imitators was William Griffin, whose 'The Lion Off Goole' shows a scene of activity in the Humber estuary. Another follower was Henry Redmore, whose 'Bambrough Castle' is of a sailing ship tossed on a stormy sea, the impression of a ship actually in the water portrayed most realistically.

Other marine works of note are the tempestuous 17th century 'Dutch Sailing Boats in a Rough Sea' by Ludolf Bakhuisen, 'The Four Days Battle' by William van de Velde, one of the finest of Dutch 17th century seascape painters, an 18th century picture of 'A Squadron Going to Windward' by Charles Brooking, and from this century 'The Pilot' by Norman Wilkinson. 'Galway Harbour' a modern work by Tristram Hillier, is both colourful and dreamlike.

The best of the Old Master paintings at Hull, apart from the Dutch works, are Italian. The earliest of these are 'A Bishop Saint' by the Florentine Bartolemmeo di Giovanni (late 15th century), and a 'Triptych' attributed to the Sienese artist Domenico Beccafumi (1486–1551). Of the later Italian paintings, 'Sophronia Offering Her

Antonio Canaletto, View on the Grand Canal, *c.1728*

Life' by Francesco Guardi (1712–93), recounting a biblical tale, is brilliant and vivid. Better still, though, is a *tour de force* by Antonio Canaletto, 'View on the Grand Canal', an atmospheric early work by the Venetian master renowned for his detailed, airy and sunlit townscapes of the 18th century.

The Dutch Old Master collection contains many extremely good paintings, and several great ones. 'Still Life' by Pieter Janssens Elinga, 'Vanitas' by Cornelis Norbertus Gysbrechts and 'Still Life in Garden' by Adriaen Gryef are all still life paintings in contrasting styles. Vanitas pictures were popular works, reminders of the transcience of life. Gysbrechts's painting is a *trompe-l'oeil*, the canvas seemingly falling from its supporting stretcher to emphasise the mortality message.

Jacob van Ruisdael was the supreme Dutch 17th century landscape painter, responsible for changing the approach of other Dutch artists, and later French and English ones, to the subject. 'Wooded Landscape with a Cornfield' is a striking example of his work. 'Winter Landscape' by Claes Molenaer is a much busier scene than Ruisdael's, with a frozen stretch of water, the local people going about their various businesses.

Church interiors were also a favourite subject in Dutch art. 'Antwerp Cathedral' by Pieter Neefs is one such work, but along with most others of the type is overwhelmed by the stunning 'Interior of St Laurens-kerk, Rotterdam' by Daniel de Blieck. This glows with light, and is painted in superb detail, down to bare patches on the walls where the plaster has fallen away. 'Supper at Emmaus' by Crijn Hendricksz. Volmarijn is a study in light and shadow, the illumination of the risen Christ and his followers coming from hidden candles.

Four Dutch 17th century paintings serve to lead us into the remarkable sequence of portraits at the Ferens. The earliest is 'Portrait of Frans van

Arthur Devis, Sir George and Lady Strickland in the Grounds of Boynton Hall, Bridlington, *1751*

Limborch' by Thomas de Keyser, painted in close detail, especially the hands and face. 'Portrait of a Young Girl' is an elegant, precise work by Bartholomeus van der Helst, more popular than Rembrandt among some quarters in his time. A portrait by Adrian Hanneman is thought by some to be that of the famous Hull poet and politician, Andrew Marvell.

The fourth portrait of this Dutch group is by a very great master, and represents the height of achievement among paintings in this region. This is 'Portrait of a Young Woman' by Frans Hals. His was a prodigious talent: his dazzling brushwork, vivacity, incredible sensitivity and insight are all seen here at their best. The painting is one of Britain's greatest treasures.

The delicate and finely-detailed 'Sir George and Lady Strickland in the Grounds of Boynton Hall, Bridlington' by Arthur Devis, and the powerful and perceptive 'Portrait of a Lady' attributed to William Hogarth, are two of the outstanding 18th century portraits, both contrasting in style with John Hoppner's slightly later one of 'Anna Isabella Milbanke', later Lady Byron, which is softer and more romanticised.

A fascinating series of 19th and 20th century portraits of women includes 'Study of a Young Woman' by Thomas Cooper Gotch, with rich patterning of the background and the subject's dress contrasting with the smooth fragility of her face. The Inter-War period produced 'Portrait of Elizabeth Allhusen' by Edmund Dulac, better known for his evocative book illustrations; the enigmatic 'A Game of Patience' by Meredith Frampton (colour plate 9); and the realistic 'By the Hills' by Gerald Brockhurst, featuring the glamorous professional actress and model, Lady Marguerite Strickland. A more recent painting is 'Portrait of Maureen Lipman', the Hull actress, by Humphrey Ocean.

Male portraits show a similar intriguing range of characterisation. 'Mr Wyndham Lewis as a Tyro' is an alarming self-portrait by Percy Wyndham Lewis (1882–1957). 'Life Painting for Myself' is a notable early work by David Hockney, while 'Self Portrait

Daniel de Blieck, Interior of St Laurenskerk, Rotterdam, *c.1655*

Frans Hals, Portrait of a Young Woman, *c.1655–60*

castings from a scrapped piano by Eduardo Paolozzi. 'Man with Cloths' is a life-sized figure in polyester resin and fibreglass by John Davies, very human, but also eerie and unreal.

Both in the range and quality of its collections, the Ferens is a jewel of an art gallery.

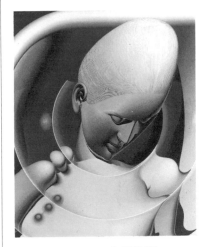

Victor Newsome, Untitled, *1980/81*

Looking Up' is a virile study by Leon Kossoff. 'The Lettermen' by Peter Blake, a large-scale painting of a 1960s American pop group, is based on a record-sleeve illustration.

Beyond maritime subjects, Old Masters and portraits, there are enormously rich collections at the Ferens. 'Cloud Study' by John Constable, 'Caldecot Castle, Monmouthshire' attributed to Thomas Girtin, and 'Croyland Abbey' by John Sell Cotman are typical, calm English early 19th century works. High Victorian drama is represented by 'Ulysses and the Sirens', with its muscular men and sylph-like sirens, by Herbert James Draper. Victorian sentimentality and coy eroticism are seen in 'Tickling the Sleeper' by Théodore Gérard. A beautiful late Impressionist painting is

'Boulogne Sands' by Philip Wilson Steer.

The 20th century paintings cover virtually the whole range of British art, including the Camden Town Group, with works such as 'Hotel Royale, Dieppe' by Walter Sickert and 'Cinema Interior' by Malcolm Drummond. Among more recent paintings are 'Building Site, Victoria Street' by Frank Auerbach, and 'Untitled' by Victor Newsome, a sci-fi image bursting from the picture.

Britain's foremost 20th century sculptors are represented in the gallery's collections, with the bronze 'Draped Torso' by Henry Moore, 'Icon II', a marble by Barbara Hepworth, and the lovely and powerful 'Isobel' by Jacob Epstein. 'Frog II' is a dumpy bronze monster made from

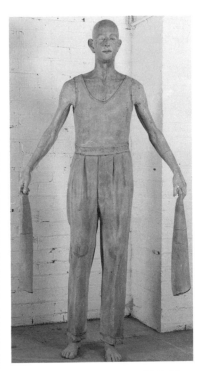

John Davies, Man with Cloths, *1974–75*

Town Docks Museum

Queen Victoria Square, Hull, North Humberside HU1 3DX
(0482) 222737
Open daily. **F** ▣
&.**S**: wheelchair access to ground floor only at present; lift to first floor to be available by late 1989.
🏥 & 🚻 advance booking preferred: contact Curator. ☺

The tragic story of Hull's whaling industry is among the most moving of the many tales told in the region's museums. This story begins and ends with the pitiable skeletons of whales, majestic denizens of the world's oceans, and the largest exhibits among what are the best maritime collections on the east coast, in this ancient port of Kingston upon Hull.

'There is a Leviathanic Museum, they tell me, in Hull, England . . . . . where they have some fine specimens of fin-backs and other whales.' So wrote Herman Melville in his great novel, *Moby Dick*, in 1851. Two of the whale skeletons referred to by Melville survive to this day in the Town Docks Museum. These are of the Bottlenose Whale, and of the Narwhal or 'sea unicorn'. The Narwhal carries a single long tusk, and whalers killed them for their tusks to bring to Hull as curios. Two matching tusks in the Town Docks Museum were used as bed posts, others were used to make hat stands. In medieval times the tusks were thought to be the horns of the fabulous unicorn, and later to have aphrodisiac qualities.

The Killer Whale is a toothed whale that hunts in packs of up to sixty in search of prey such as squid, fish and seals (twenty-four seals have been found in one Killer Whale's stomach). Killers may have twenty-eight teeth in each jaw, as seen in the museum's skeleton. The Sperm Whale is also toothed, but is much larger, growing up to sixty-five feet long and weighing fifty tons. Its size is indicated by the immense jaw in the museum.

It was the Greenland Right Whale that was hunted by the Hull whalers for its oil. It was a slow swimmer, docile, and reached fifty tons in weight. The museum has a forty-foot, two-year-old female Southern Right Whale skeleton, a cousin of the Greenland Right Whale, which has now been hunted to the verge of extinction, and which is represented here by a massive vertebra formerly used as a butcher's chopping block.

Baleen is the fibrous horny material in the Right Whale's jaws, which acts as a sieve through which the whale separates food from sea water. Baleen, bone and teeth were all used by whalers to make 'useful' items, such as walking sticks, umbrellas, stay busks, teething rings, necklets, combs, brooms and brushes. The museum also has specimens of sperm oil, whale liver oil and krill (whale food) in spirit.

The fearsome weaponry of the whaler ranged from hand-held harpoons, to whaling crossbows, harpoon guns, electric harpoons and obscene explosive harpoons. A huge blubber pot was used to heat blubber, to extract the valuable oil, once it had been cut from the whale's carcase using a variety of 'flensing' blades. Special grips were worn on shoes to aid walking on the slippery skin of whales during flensing.

A fine series of whaling ship models includes the 'Harpooner' of Whitby, built in the 18th century, and the 'Swan' of Hull, which survived the Davis Straits disaster of 1830 when nineteen British ships were lost in the ice. In 1836, the 'Swan' was again trapped in Baffin Bay, and twenty-five crewmen died of frostbite, starvation and scurvy. One model whale boat is made from a Sperm Whale jaw.

Two famous whaling ships are prominent. The 'Truelove' was built in 1764, and saw action as a privateer in the American War of Independence before becoming a Hull whaler. Between 1784 and 1868, 'Truelove' made a staggering seventy-two voyages to the Arctic, capturing over 400 whales. Relics of 'Truelove' include plaster casts of an Eskimo couple, brought to Hull on the vessel in 1847, an octant and harpoons. The 'Diana' was one of the last Hull whaling vessels, and it was hoped that she would revive the dying trade when she sailed to the Arctic in

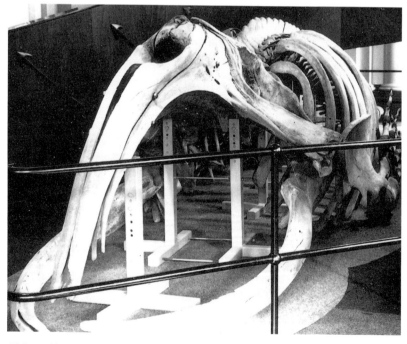

Skeleton of female Southern Right Whale

The 'Tyr' cutting across a British warship during the Cod War, 1975

brought back by Hull whalers. A polar bear and bear cub skeleton are other mementoes.

Whaling art ranges from the serene paintings of John Ward (1798–1849), such as 'The "Swan" and "Isabella"', and other works by Robert Willoughby (1768–1843) and Thomas Binks (1799–1852), to the beautiful and uniquely important 'scrimshaw' collections. These are carvings made by sailors on whale teeth and bones, and walrus tusks.

The rise of Hull's fishing industry followed the decline of whaling after 1836, caused by the decline in numbers of northern whales, and is well chronicled in the museum. Models show the different methods of deep sea and inshore fishing. Outstanding among these are the 'Specimen', a Hull smack built in 1879, and the 'Boston Seafire', a 1948 steam trawler, which was the first British trawler to be fitted with radar. Push the button and plunge the model into inky darkness!

An extraordinary incident occurred in 1904 when the tiny vessels of the Hull Gamecock Fleet, trawling on Dogger Bank, were confronted by Russian warships on their way to the Far East to fight the Japanese. The trawlers sent up warning rockets to avoid a collision, but the Russians,

Eskimo dolls

cines, a pair of Eskimo baby's boots, and a seal-pick.

An Eskimo Kayak, sealskins, boots, weapons, models and toys (with dolls, carvings, and an igloo complete with miniature family) are more items

the 1860s. Instead, she was caught in the ice in 1866, and thirteen men died, including the captain. 'Diana' was wrecked in 1869. From 'Diana' come an ancient and wormeaten ship's biscuit, a journal kept by the ship's surgeon on the agonising 1866–67 voyage, an 1859 log book, ship's medi-

Figurehead from the transatlantic paddlesteamer, 'Syrius'

fearing attack, opened fire, sinking the 'Crane'. A portion of the 'Mino''s companionway survives, riddled with holes from the Russian shelling. The Russian fleet was eventually obliterated by the Japanese Navy, which had more to offer than the fish waved by the Hull trawlermen to show the jumpy Russian sailors who they were.

By 1920 Hull's trawlers had over-fished the North Sea, and they moved north to the Faroe Islands and Iceland, and later went further afield to the Barents Sea, Newfoundland and Greenland. In both the First and Second World Wars, Hull's trawlers were requisitioned by the Royal Navy for minesweeping and anti-submarine duties, depicted in splendid photographs and paintings. When Iceland extended her fishing limits from twelve to 200 miles in 1975, the Cod War resulted, with hostilities involving British and Icelandic warships, and Hull trawlers. A model of the 'Arctic Corsair', shelled in the Cod War, is on view.

Displays on the Humber Estuary show the constant battle to survey, dredge and navigate this treacherous stretch of water. Models of the Bull and Spurn Lightships represent the elaborate warning system. The real Spurn Lightship can be seen and boarded in Hull's Marina a couple of hundred yards away (admission free).

The museum's collections also feature a wide range of other items, such as a medieval dugout, ships' figureheads (notably a black dog from the transatlantic paddlesteamer 'Sirius'), French prisoner-of-war models, navigation instruments, a superb series of marine paintings, a boarding axe used aboard HMS 'Victory' at Trafalgar, a model of the Hull-built 'Bethia', later called the 'Bounty', uniforms from the Trinity House Navigation School, and various items of maritime-related decorative art.

If you have any salt in your veins, have any sympathy with the plight of whales (they are still hunted commercially), or have ever wondered what the difference is between a cod and a haddock, you must visit the Town Docks Museum in Hull.

Transport and Archaeology Museums

36 High Street, Hull, North Humberside HU1 1NQ
(0482) 222737
Open daily. **F P** &
⛑ & ⛑ advance booking
preferred: contact Curator. ☺

Hewn from a single gigantic oak tree, the spectacular prehistoric Hasholme Boat looms out of the mist inside its experimental Boatlab, entombed there until the year 2000. It is one of many fascinating exhibits among the best archaeology collections in the North, which share a building – Hull's old Corn Exchange – with a large number of outstanding vehicles and transport items in an expanding museum complex.

400 years before the birth of Christ a heavy cargo boat foundered on the River Foulness, loaded with timber and beef. 2,300 years later the sunken vessel was discovered by pure chance during drainage works in a field near the modern course of the Foulness. In an audacious operation, the waterlogged boat, known as the Hasholme Boat, was recovered, and is now undergoing conservation in Hull designed to stablise her without distortion caused by drying out.

The massive oak tree from which the Hasholme Boat was created was 800 years old when felled, and eighty feet high. No oak in the world today approaches that size. This is Britain's largest prehistoric boat, an astonishing

Boatlab with Hasholme Boat

Roman portrait on wall plaster from Brantingham

monument to Iron-Age technology, and a compelling link with the past.

A thirty-year-old man, buried around 200 BC at Garton Slack, is now immortalised in the museum because his was the first chariot burial ever recovered successfully in this country. The man was buried crouched upon the remains of his chariot, the bronze and iron 'nave' bands and iron tyres of which survived across the centuries, with the metal cylinder from the stock of his whip. Also found in the grave was a decapitated pig, its skull cleft in two as part of the pagan burial ritual.

Venus, goddess of Love, attended by a Triton or Merman, is the central figure of the famous 'Venus Mosaic', one of a beautiful series of Roman mosaics at Hull, which is unparalleled in this country. Venus holds a golden apple in one hand, and a mirror is falling from the other. Birds, animals, naked hunters and Mercury all feature in the mosaic, which is dated to around 350–361 AD, and was found in a Roman house at Rudston.

The Brantingham 'Tyche Mosaic' of 330–350 AD has as its centrepiece a representation of a bust wearing a crown, the towers of which identify it as a Tyche, or figure representing a town or province. Wall plaster also found at Brantingham carries a strikingly modern portrait of a woman, and a second mosaic follows a geometric pattern. Fish and sea monsters, lotuses and trees adorn the 'Aquatic Mosaic' of 350–361 AD, which formed part of the *apodyterium* or undressing room of a bath suite at Rudston.

Unique in Britain is the 'Charioteer Mosaic', also from Rudston, of the early 4th century AD. The centre panel depicts a victorious charioteer standing in his four-horse chariot, holding symbols of victory – a palm and a wreath. Female busts represent the four seasons, Spring with a swallow on her shoulder, Summer with poppies in her hair.

'Orpheus Charming the Animals' is one of a group of three mosaics discovered at Horkstow. Orpheus is playing his lyre in a central roundel, with animals – elephant, bear, boar and hound hunting a deer – enchanted by his music and voice. The 'Chariot Race' is the second Horkstow mosaic, featuring four two-horse chariots hurtling around a race track. Only a fragment of the third mosaic survives.

The Roman mosaics are complemented by a very fine collection of other local material from the period of the Roman occupation of Britain. Tiny lacrymatory bottles were for funeral mourners to gather tears to bury with the dead. Superb bronze statuettes of Venus and Hercules are of a type kept in a small household shrine in the 2nd and 3rd century AD. A statuette of an actor wears a Greek robe and a wide-mouthed mask to indicate a comic character. Bracelets of amber beads and bronze, fragments of a blue and white glass bracelet, enamelled brooches, finger rings, and bronze and bone hair pins are some of the items of jewellery. Objects from a priest's burial include small ceremonial sceptres, which were bent before burial to kill their power. Cosmetic bottles, ear picks, wheat from an army depot, a cheese press, a strainer, bronze spoons, a huge coin hoard hidden around 334 AD, a tiny bronze model anvil, and a name stamp used for marking goods

Hansom cab of G. Richardson & Son

such as eye ointment, show the diversity of these collections. Anglian burial urns from a pagan cemetary at Sanction are probably those of mercenaries hired by the native British to protect them from other marauding Angles after the Romans withdrew from the region.

In addition to the archaeology collections, the museum complex houses Hull's transport collections. The oldest form of transport in the museum are sedan chairs of about 1800. Next come a horsedrawn sleigh of 1810, and a dandy horse or draisine of 1818. This is a forerunner of the bicycle used by the outsize Reverend Joseph Coltman, Curate of Beverley Minster, said to have weighed over thirty-seven stone. Other early vehicles are a Britzschka carriage and an elegant Cabriolet, both of 1820, and a Travelling Chariot of 1825.

One of the great strengths of the transport collections are the Victorian horsedrawn vehicles. A Road Coach of 1860 looks as if it came straight out of a John Wayne film, and could carry up to twenty-two people in all. Another large, heavy vehicle is a grand State or Dress Coach of 1860. A fashionable, light Barouche of 1862, a Landau of 1868, a Brougham of 1880 and a Victoria of 1880 are classic Victorian carriages.

Late Victorian public service vehicles are characterised by the Hansom Cab. The early, cumbersome Hansoms were unsteady and unpopular, but by 1889 they had developed into the

Detail of the early 4th century Charioteer Mosaic from Rudston

Sturmey Voiturette, 1900

An extensive collection of bicycles, tricycles and motorcycles, petrol pumps (one of them, marked Russian Oil Products, looking for all the world like a lighthouse), transport uniforms, AA badges, car horns, and a large and impressive collection of horse brasses are among the many other transport treasures.

Both Archaeology and Transport collections are undergoing radical re-display, and more is coming onto view all the time in a group of old and new buildings on Hull's historic High Street.

Road Coach, 1860

charming bow-fronted vehicles like that owned by G. Richardson & Son of Hull. There is little similarity, though, between the bow-fronted model and the bizarre three-wheeled hansom of about 1900, said to have been used by Edward VII. A wagonette-brake of 1895 was another popular form of public transport.

Veteran cars are also strongly represented in Hull. A Panhard et Levassor Motor Wagonette of 1899 is upright and solid. This is very similar to the model that won the 1,050 mile Paris to Marseilles race in 1896. A Daimler of 1899 is more low-slung, and established the reputation of Daimler for workmanship and reliability. A Sturmey Voiturette of 1900 (using an air-cooled motorcycle engine), a Gardner-Serpollet Steam Car of 1901, a White Stanhope Steam Car of 1901, and a Marshall-Benz Vis à Vis of 1901 are all important vehicles. The aristocrat among the veterans, though, is the majestic yellow Lanchester Open Tourer of 1907/8 – luxury on wheels!

The world's oldest tramcar is here too, having survived being pushed through some buffer stops and dam-aged in 1935. This is the famous Ryde Pier tram, built in 1871. The Kitson steam tram locomotive is another rare vehicle, of 1882. A Hull Corporation tram of 1910 brings the story of tramways into the 20th century.

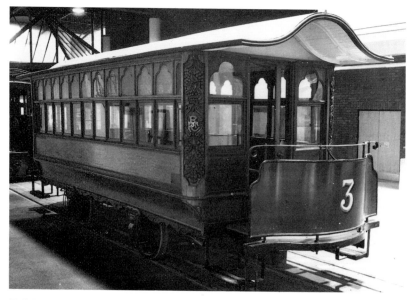

Ryde Pier tram, 1871

Wilberforce House and Georgian Houses

High Street, Hull, North Humberside, HU1 1NE (0482) 222737
Open daily. 🇫 🇵
♿ **S**: wheelchair access to ground floor only.
🎫 & 🍴 advance booking preferred.

By the 19th century over ten million human beings had been forcibly taken from their West-African villages to be sold into slavery on the West Indies plantations. Lives were ruined, families were destroyed, vast fortunes were made. The traffic in slaves was the most shameful of all methods of exploitation of the African peoples by West Europeans.

This unique museum was the birthplace of William Wilberforce (1759–1833), who fought the slave trade and eventually brought about its abolition. Its collections record the trade, the desperate struggle to crush it, and Wilberforce's eventual success. The museum also contains a variety of other material, notably 17th and 18th century decorative art and furnishings, and a superb collection of dolls.

The horrors of the slave trade are brought home indelibly by the shackles and chains used to fetter the Africans. The most chilling of these is the iron collar with four two-foot-long spikes to prevent the wearer making an escape. A ring and staple was used for chaining slaves in a stockade or barracoon at Lekki in Africa. Gang chains were for securing groups of slaves, silver branding irons for marking them in just the same way as farmers brand cattle.

The use of branding iron and chains is illustrated in the painting 'Scene on the Coast of Africa' by A.F. Biard. This portrays Africans selling their own kind to white slavers, and the use of whips to control the unwilling cargo. Other scenes of slave traffic are depicted on ivory tusks of the 19th century.

The trade in human bondage was based on various commodities, such as

Effigy of William Wilberforce

pepper, ivory and gold. Bars of iron, brass and copper, known as 'manellas', were used as money in West Africa.

The slave trade is also recorded in documents. There is a broadsheet of around 1700 by the Royal African Company against Parliament's breaking of its slave trade monopoly, and a letter of 1759 to the captain of the slave ship, 'Nancy', from her London shipowners. A slave trader's log book is dated 1764.

More graphic is a list of slaves who died on board the ship 'Katherine' in 1728. The causes of death given are 'flux', 'jumped overboard', 'sullen and malloncholly', 'feavour', 'suddenly', and others. Many slave ships carried a surgeon, who lost money if deaths occurred among the cargo.

The most prized exhibit is the actual slave-ship model that Wilberforce used in the House of Commons to demonstrate the horrific conditions endured by the Africans while at sea. The model is of the Liverpool ship 'Brookes', of 320 tons.

Further degradation followed for the Africans after they had crossed the Atlantic. An auction bill of 1828 records for sale Sarah, aged about fourteen, and Jack Antonia, aged about forty, along with rice, grain, books, muslins, needles, pins, ribbons and the horse Blucher. An inventory of the

Valley Plantation, St John's Jamaica, of 1787 lists women ('Patience, Elderly feild Negroe' worth £50), girls ('Rose, Infant' worth £20, 'Sally, Infant' worth £5), and invalids ('Katy, Blind' worth £6); then follows a schedule of livestock, oxen, a bull and cows.

The 1828 punishment records of the Sarah Plantation in British Guiana carefully lists the slaves who were whipped over a six month period. In all thirty-two slaves, men and women, received 499 lashes. Some of the whips used on slaves are displayed. Runaways were not tolerated. A runaway poster of 1838 from Kentucky offered a reward of between fifty and 150 dollars for the capture of Henry May, a twenty-two year old runaway, who functioned as a dining room servant before making his bid for freedom.

The anti-slavery movement in England produced propaganda in the form of caricatures, broadsheets, pottery and medallions. Examples of all these restore one's faith in human nature, even in the 18th and 19th centuries. One jug bears the message: 'Remember them that are in Bonds / Oh! Women of England, your influence extend, / Ye Mothers, ye Daughters, the helpless defend, / These strong ties are sever'd for one crime alone, / Possessing a Colour less fair than your own.'

These immensely important and

Anti-slavery caricature, published in 1792

Group of anti-slavery ceramics

are full of fascinating collections. The oak-panelled banqueting room and bedroom contain 17th century furniture, pewter and paintings. There is also an outstanding collection of dummy boards, the original function of which were as fire screens. These depict nursemaids and children, gardeners with spades, and a soldier. In the bedroom hang portraits of Andrew Marvell, the 17th century Hull poet and politician.

Among the 18th century furniture and furnishings, one of the best items is a Sheraton reading chair with adjustable bookrest. A sculptor's model of a statue of King William III, the full-size version of which stands in Hull's city centre, is by Peter Scheemakers, and is of the early 18th century. The most exceptional exhibit is a carved and painted wooden figure of a negro servant in 18th century costume. This is supposed to have come from the Pump Room at Bath.

Figure of a negro servant

rare collections include personal items that belonged to Wilberforce, the champion of the anti-slavery movement. A painting, 'Slave in Chains' by Thomas Barker (1769–1847) is a moving representation of a black slave dressed in red, the light reflecting from his manacles. This was used by Wilberforce in his lectures on emancipation.

Wilberforce House dates from the middle of the 17th century, and with the neighbouring 18th century buildings comprises a complex of rooms that

Group of Hull silver

Two more specialist collections are of enormous interest. One of these is of dolls, of which Wilberforce House has a great number. Dolls have been made for thousands of years, and have been produced commercially since the 14th century, although they have not always been merely toys. They come in all sorts of shapes, sizes and materials – wood, china, wax, 'composition', celluloid, rag, plastic. Some Russian moss men in the collection are made from moss and wood. A sacrificial doll from Korea is made of straw. Scottish dolls; a Golliwog; a Suffragette rag doll; dolls dressed as sailors; a German doll dressed as a fisherman in oilskin coat, hat and waders; an Irish doll with a pig, and many more, cover a huge range. The most spectacular dolls are the 19th century Hina-Matsuiri models of the Emperor and Empress of Japan attended by their officials, ladies of the court and musicians, with furniture and other miniature items.

The famous Hull silver on display dates from the 17th century, when the city had its own assay office. Among the spoons, cups and goblets, the most beautiful pieces are the tankards, with their pierced and engraved decoration.

Firearms and costume are other strong collections, and together with a chemist's shop, Heal's furniture, military displays and Victorian parlour, they make for a most varied, atmospheric museum, with something new at every turn. You can even sit out in the gardens under the mulberry tree, and watch the river Hull glide by, where merchants and whalers once unloaded their vessels.

HUTTON-LE-HOLE

Ryedale Folk Museum

Hutton-le-Hole, North Yorkshire YO6 6UA   (07515) 367
Closed November to mid-March.
🅿
& ST: wheelchair access to many parts, although some steps between levels; upper floors of buildings inaccessible.
🚹 & 🚺 reduced admission rates for pre-booked parties. ☼

Hutton-le-Hole nestles in the valley of Hutton Beck in the North York Moors. This pretty village is an attraction in itself, and the presence there since 1964 of the Ryedale Folk Museum has added to the number of people eager to wend their way into this unspoilt area.

The Ryedale Museum's collections derive mostly from the area around Hutton, which remains as it has always been, rural in character. These collections, with those of **Beck Isle Museum** in nearby Pickering, provide us with marvellous insights into the nature of North Yorkshire rural life before the Second World War. This is all the more notable because the area has very rich local traditions, and to many it represents the essential Yorkshire.

Ryedale's buildings are its most obvious assets. They are twelve in number, if we include the witch's hovel (!), and all contain items from the museum's collections. The most remarkable of these is the Elizabethan stone-built manor house, brought to Hutton from the village of Harome in 1971–72. It is of cruck construction, the crucks being the largest yet discovered in North Yorkshire. The manor house doubled as a family home for the Lord of the Manor, and as the meeting hall for Harome Manor Court.

The manor house contains a bizarre mixture of material, ranging from a lock and key from Neville Castle to an Egyptian horseshoe for work in the desert. At the time I visited there was a collection of local archaeological finds on display, including Anglo-Saxon and Viking carved stones, which are so familiar in the area, and Romano-British finds from Spaunton; there were also lots of flints and pottery, and an Anglo-Saxon carpenter's axe. (The archaeological items are currently

Exterior view of the Elizabethan Manor House from Harome

Interior view of the Manor House, showing cruck construction

John Wrightson of Stokesley in the late 18th century. When in his counselling room he dressed in a long robe with a strange headcovering, the aura of the necromancer reinforced by his mysterious preparations, dried herbs, skull and globe.

The theme of witchcraft continues in the reconstructed Stang End thatched cruck house of 1704, rebuilt here in 1967. In the hearth is another witch-post, this *in situ* to protect against witchcraft. The witch-post became a powerful talisman in the North York Moors, its cross and other markings said to have been carved by a priest, and once the house's occupants were past the witch-post they were safe from harm. This building contains a collection of grease-horns, drenching horns and tumblers made from cattle horns, some honest oak country furniture, and domestic items, such as a cheese press, loom, spinning wheel, bee skeps and a verjuice press for crushing crab apples.

Harome Cottage was rebuilt here in 1974, and has rooms laid out as kitchen, living room and dairy, furnished in traditional farm fashion – copper kettles, brass pans, windsor chair, child's high chair, Staffordshire dogs, Family Bible, and a Thomas Fletcher (of Kirkbymoorside) longcase clock. Of particular interest is a lacemaker's candlestool with its glass globes, and an old Merrills board (Nine Men's Morris). This is a reminder that the museum actually hosts the Merrills World Championships every year.

Another building houses reconstructed 'craftshops' – a tinsmith, boot

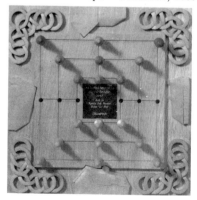

Merrills board

being relocated.) A display of treen features a nice set of knitting sheaths, with butter moulds, potato mashers and Gypsy pegs. A church clock from Guisborough was made by a blacksmith in the 16th century.

Not surprisingly for an area so steeped in superstition, there is a section dealing with witchcraft. This includes a witch's Garter Book for forecasting the future, and a copy of a Magic Book used with dice and a spin-wheel by Peggy Devell, a witch of Hutton-le-Hole of the 17th-18th centuries. Witch stones, a witch-post from Rosedale, a witch's bottle, a witch-charm from Sheriff Hutton, and a witch's crystal from Ebberstone indicate the widespread nature of belief in witchcraft, whether for good or for evil. The most famous wise man or magician of the area is said to have been

19th century Threshing machine by Marshalls of Gainsborough

JARROW

The Bede Monastery Museum

Jarrow Hall, Church Bank, Jarrow, Tyne and Wear NE32 3DY
(091) 489 2106
Closed Mondays. ▯ ▣ ℙ
& S: ramp at side door for wheelchair access via café; stairs to upper floor but assistance given to lift chairs.
▥ contact Curator or Receptionist in advance; ▥ contact Education team. Book as far in advance as possible (bookings have to be confirmed with church).
For St Paul's Church contact Rev. R Corker, St Peter's House, York Avenue, Jarrow (091) 489 0946.

and shoe maker, cooper, cabinet-maker (with very fine inlaid tool chest), saddler, iron foundry, wheelwright and chemist. The latter features mysterious-sounding names on the drug drawers: Fuscus Van., Rad. Rhei, P. Carbo.Lig, Pulv.S.Anisi. More self-explanatory are the Rayglo laxative tablets and some other palliatives mercifully long out of use.

In a barn, a crofter's cottage and the 'helm shed' are some of the museum's farming collections. The threshing machine is a pre-1870 model by Marshalls of Gainsborough, on wooden wheels. Two Yorkshire wagons, one a Moors wagon, the other a Dales wagon, can be seen alongside other farm vehicles. Forks, flails, rakes, a winnowing machine, a 'tip' reaper by Bamletts of Thirsk, a woodbeam plough by Hornshaws of Dunnington, and lots more implements testify to the underlying nature of the local economy.

A unique reconstructed Elizabethan glass furnace, a pottery kiln, and displays on iron mining, the Rosedale railway and the local tile industry show that not everybody, even in this most rural of rural areas, derived their livings from farming and associated crafts.

Miscellaneous items around the museum's two and a half acre site include a double stocks, an unusual stone for shaping hazel oxbows (ox collars), a maypole, the first tractor in the district (a Fordson of the 1930s), stone rollers, a Gypsy caravan, a rather grand horsedrawn hearse, millstones, a working blacksmith's forge, and a barn threshing-machine with horsewheel.

Finally, the entrance building houses domestic items which illustrate the daily chores of washing, cleaning and ironing before electricity lightened the burden. Good small displays of horse brasses, lacemaking and lighting lead on to some charming dolls' houses, and toys and dolls. A map of 'Israel As divided among the Tribes', dated 1856, survives to ensure a version of immortality for its small creator, Master A. Weetman of Appleton-le-Moors District School (colour plate 1). Here too is perhaps the best piece of all in the museum – a brass and timber water clock inscribed 'Joseph Ellsworth of ye towne Coatbridge AD 1635'. Its accompanying water trough bears a message for all of us: 'As tyme & houres passeth awaye / So doeth ye lite of man decaye / As tyme can be redeemed with no coste / Bestowe it well & let no houre be loste.'

1,300 years ago was born a man whose writings were to have a profound influence on the western world, which is still felt today. He was a monk named Bede, and he lived and died at the monastery of St Paul at Jarrow.

This unusual little museum is sited in Jarrow Hall, just 300 yards from St Paul's Church, the chancel of which is the actual church where Bede worshipped in the 7th and 8th centuries AD. Both buildings have relics of life in St Paul's monastery during and since that time. Adjacent to the church are the excavated remains of the rest of the monastery, and of Anglo-Saxon and later buildings.

The monastery of St Paul was founded in 682 AD by monks from the nearby monastery of St Peter at Monkwearmouth. The two houses functioned together as a single monastery. St Paul's church was built of stone, much of it taken from abandoned Roman buildings in the vicinity. At least some of its windows held stained glass, produced in workshops on the site. The church was dedicated to God's glory on 23rd April 685. The dedication inscription survives to this day in the wall of the church, while some of

Exterior view of Jarrow Hall

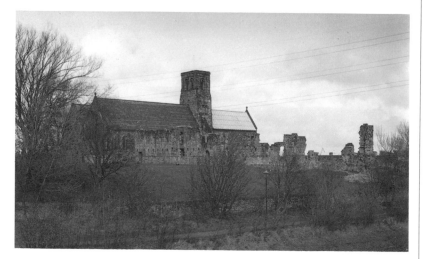

View of St Paul's Church and remains of St Paul's monastery

and began his education there in 680 at the age of seven. Inspired by the library collected together in Europe by the founder of the twin monastery, Benedict Biscop, Bede and other scholars established Jarrow as one of Europe's greatest centres of learning, celebrated throughout the known world. Among Bede's own works are fifty of biblical commentary, lives of abbots and saints, treatises in Time, Mathematics and Poetry, and the immortal *History of the English Church and People*.

Other famous books produced by Jarrow and Monkwearmouth monks in their *scriptorium* include three massive copies of the Bible, completed before 716 AD when one copy was taken to Rome. Of the three, only the Roman copy survives complete. This is the *Codex Amiatinus*, which is in the Laurentian Library in Florence.

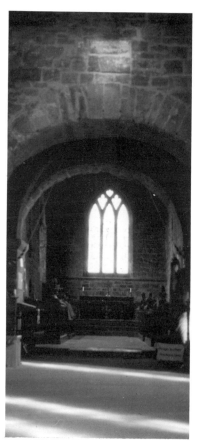

Interior view, St Paul's Church

the stained glass can be seen both in the museum, and beautifully restored in a unique round window in the church. This is the oldest stained glass in England.

The church also has a collection of carved stones from the original 7th century building, which were discovered during a 19th century restoration. These include the Jarrow Cross (late 7th/early 8th century), and friezes of the same date carved with plant scroll, originally used to decorate the church, which would have been brought to the monastery for use as building stone. The museum has more fragments of the early monastery, notably some stone roof slabs, and re-used Roman wares, including roof-tiles used by the monks to form a drain at the end of the refectory.

Bede, known as the 'Venerable', was born in 673 AD near the site of St Peter's monastery, Monkwearmouth,

Horse's head corbel, 11th century

Leaves from one of the lost volumes have been found, one in 1889 in a Newcastle antiquarian shop (it had been used as a wrapper for some 18th century accounts), and eleven more in 1911 (which had been used as wrappers for estate papers at Wollaton Hall in Nottinghamshire). A further leaf, probably from the third Bible, turned up as recently as 1982, this time wrapping deeds in Dorset. Further leaves probably await discovery.

The museum has examples of styli, and a bone-handled point that may have been used in the scriptorium. It also has other personal items, such as whetstones, combs and leather-working tools, found on the monastery site. There are Anglo-Saxon coins (sceattas and stycas), a harp or lyre peg, a hollow bone tube, which is perhaps the mouthpiece of a musical instrument, and glass-making equipment. These are tantalising glimpses of a world very ordinary but at the same time very mysterious and different from our own.

Miscellaneous finds from the monastery that are on display in the museum include more coins, mostly medieval; 8th to 16th century pottery; a 13th century amber seal depicting a dove with an olive branch; a 16th century seal, possibly of a merchant; a tiny ivory box; and a lovely stone corbel in the shape of a horse's head, of the 11th century. There are also keys, buttons, buckles, rings, a spear-head and knife handles.

Long said to have been Bede's Chair is an admittedly very old wooden chair now in St Paul's Church. There is no

Bede's Chair, St Paul's Church

reason to suppose that Bede, an ordinary monk, had his own chair, and as others contents of the monastery have been destroyed, much of them by fire, it is rather unlikely that his chair survived when all else perished. Nevertheless, the Chair is as genuine a relic as most, and has attracted pilgrims eager to be associated with the canonised Bede. In former days, pieces of the chair were picked off by pilgrims, who would then immerse the pieces in water, which they would drink so as to cure their ailments. This was as likely to work as many other medieval cures.

Bede himself is not buried at St Paul's, where he died in 735 AD. His bones were stolen by a Durham cleric named Alfred Westou around 1020 ('Durham Steals Bede's Bones' proclaims the museum's graphic panel!), and were placed in the tomb of St Cuthbert in Durham. The bones were returned briefly in 1069, when Bishop of Durham fled from William the Conqueror, carrying St Cuthbert's coffin with him, along with Bede's remains. Nevertheless, the spirit of the Venerable Bede lingers on in Jarrow, once the intellectual centre of Europe.

KEIGHLEY

Cliffe Castle

Spring Gardens Lane, Keighley, West Yorkshire BD20 6LH
(0274) 758230
Closed Mondays. 🄵 🄼 🄿
♿ **ST**: wheelchair access to ground floor only.
🚻 & ♥ welcome, phone in advance; contact Educational staff to book an educational visit or take part in organised events. ◎

Birds, bees, bats, baryte, brachiopods, bells, baby clothes – all of these can be found in the Gothic splendour of Cliffe Castle, the setting for some fine collections, particularly of natural history and local history, with decorative art to broaden the appeal.

Among the oldest exhibits in any museum are fossils, the remains of once flourishing forms of life, most of which died out many millions of years ago, to be replaced by 'superior' species. Fossils of arthropods and brachiopods are, at up to 500 million years old, unimaginably ancient. The geological periods, Cambrian, Ordovician, Silurian, Devonian, Carboniferous, Permian and Triassic, bring us to 200 million years ago. By this time fish had appeared in the seas, represented here by a fossil of *Palaeoniscus*.

The Triassic period saw the appearance of the first true dinosaurs. The footprint of the reptile *Cheirotherium* is of this era. A reptilian vertebra of the Jurassic period, and the spines of *Cidaris* of the Cretaceous period leads us up to (only) sixty-five million years ago.

Different habitats gave rise to different plants and animals, reflected in the fossil record. From the Carboniferous Limestone seas come trilobites and gastropods. From the swamps come fin spines, shark teeth and the sharp head spine of *Xenacanthus*. The remains of the amphibian *Pholiderpeton scutigerum Huxley* were found at Tottshaw Colliery in 1868. This was one of the first backboned animals to walk on land,

Part of the reconstruction of a Carboniferous swamp and its inhabitants

and it had sharp teeth and bony scales. A model of this creature brings an extra dimension to the fossil.

A sectioned ammonite, a nautilus shell and a conifer stem are examples of the beauty of fossils. In the conifer stem, water carrying silicates has percolated through the tree trunk and preserved the annual rings in red jasper agate.

From the Ice Age come the remains of animals more familiar to us. Teeth of horse, bison and a young 'straight-toothed' elephant, of mammoths and woolly rhinoceros are all that is left of once-mighty beasts. Skulls of brown bear and badger are later still, from the period when humans were beginning to make their presence felt on the earth.

Much older than fossils are rocks and minerals, the very stuff of which the planet is made. The lovely displays at Cliffe Castle are a fairyland of colours, textures and shapes. You can also learn a lot about the different properties of minerals.

Colour in minerals varies tremendously, and can be spectacular. Some of the more vibrant colours are blue (lazurite), yellow (sulphur), green (malachite), pink (thulite) and purple (amethyst quartz). We learn from the displays that 'lustre' is the term used to describe the surface of a mineral in reflected light: gypsum is 'silky', mica schist 'pearly', haematite 'splendant',

opal 'resinous', pyrite 'metallic'. The form of minerals can be nodular (clay ironstone), globular (zeolite), stalagtitic (chalcedony), fibrous (serpentine), prismatic (tourmaline) and cockscomb (baryte). Mineralogists live in a world full of the most amazing words!

The most sensational attribute of minerals is their fluorescence, which is the coloured luminosity produced by their absorption of ultra violet light. This gives rise to glorious displays of deep violet, green and red in particular.

Other elements of the natural world

consist of birds, insects, mammals, fish, reptiles and amphibians. Some of these to be found in the area around Keighley are displayed, among them a colourful series of butterflies, such as the small Copper and Red Admiral. Visitors more rare to the region are the Clouded Yellow, Camberwell Beauty and Dark Green Fritillary.

Twenty-nine different types of pigeon are here in a single case, near the adder, common toad, slow worm and grass snake. The Pipistrelle bat, Daubenton's bat and the Noctule bat are examples of the only mammals that are completely adapted to flight. Mammals that stick to the ground include the ferret, (domesticated by man since the 1st century BC), stoat, weasel, shrews, otter, pine marten, fox, hedgehog and mole.

A series of late 19th century period rooms contain opulent furniture and furnishings. A harp and grand piano dominate a music room, which also has a kidney-shaped love seat and several paintings, including a typical flower study by the Frenchman, Fantin Latour. A set of quartetto tables of about 1830 by Joseph Nutter of Bradford, a French cabinet of about 1770 by Martin Carlin, and a typical watercolour by John Sell Cotman of 'Croyland Abbey' are among items in the

View of rock and mineral displays at Cliffe Castle

small drawing room. A notable painting in the hall outside these two rooms is the Edwardian portrait of Pauline, Lady Astor by John Singer Sargent, whose works encapsulate that period. Another work by Cotman, this time a 'Study of a Monk' hangs in a room with 'The Bather' by William Etty, the Victorian artist best known for his paintings of nudes, and with a study of 'Richmond, Yorkshire' by Philip Wilson Steer (1860–1921). There are two female bronze figures here, a table of about 1860 by Pratt and Prince of Bradford, and a side-cabinet of about 1880 by Druce & Co of London, which is of walnut veneer inlaid with boxwood and ebony

The local history collections are displayed in the 'Bygones Room', a quaint term from the distant past! There are some witch stones, charms against evil (one of them a dried sheep or bullock heart stuck all over with pins), a crystal ball used in Blackpool (well, it's not *all* local), and witch balls. Glass walking sticks filled with hundreds-and-thousands were hung up in windows as protection against witches, who would take so long to count the sweets that dawn would break before they finished.

There are good collections of irons, lamps, lanterns, candlesticks, tinder boxes, kitchen utensils, animal bells, smoking pipes and other domestic items. Dolls, toys and games include a smashing early 20th century fort with soldiers, and a toy ferris wheel. A group of knitting sheaths showing some regional styles – Cumbrian, Durham, Weardale, Teesdale, Dentdale – while a surprising collection of musical instruments features an ophicleide, a serpent, a raft zither from Lake Chad, an early 18th century guitar by Frederick Hintz, a late 18th century French hurdy gurdy, and a set of musical glasses or hydrodaktulpsychicharmonica (!).

As if this were not enough, you can also see costume, some interesting electrotypes, displays of pottery, bees and beehives, and a conservatory, all in all making for a most varied and stimulating visit. The minerals in particular stand out as one of the best displays of the type in the region.

LEEDS
Abbey House Museum
Kirkstall, Leeds, West Yorkshire
LS5 3GH   (0532) 755821
Open daily. ▣
♿ **ST**: wheelchair access to most of ground floor only, including Norman Hall and period streets but excluding toy and costume galleries; **T** late 1989.
⚑ & ⚑ contact Museum Secretary to book. ◉

The 12th century Great Gatehouse of Kirkstall Abbey now houses a museum with collections that illustrate Leeds life in the past, and are especially strong in toys and games, and shop contents. Across the width of a dual carriageway stands the ruined Abbey itself, a virtually full-height Cistercian foundation. This once dominated the Aire Valley, and has a grandeur that ranks with the finest of monastic sites, resonant with the chastity, poverty and obedience that ruled the lives of the black-cowled Cistercians.

The museum contains a number of relics of the Abbey, which has been attracting tourists since the 18th century. Tourism encouraged the production of souvenirs, such as a moulded model of the Abbey of 1910. Tiles, masonry, bronze taps, lead piping and a 16th century chamber pot are finds from the Abbey site itself.

Dolls and dolls' houses have a long history, and come in many shapes and sizes. Among the pottery, porcelain, rag and wood dolls, one of special note is a wax doll of about 1745–55, which is dressed in a pale blue corded-silk open robe and petticoat. This was probably intended as a toy for an adult rather than a child. One tiny doll is made from a peachstone, and sits in a cradle made from a walnut shell. The dolls' houses include a 'timber-framed' one of 1883, and a huge edifice of 1870 with furniture and furnishings on three floors.

The toys and games evoke a childhood as we would all like it to have

Wax doll, c.1745–55

been. Foretelling the world of adulthood are a model theatre, a toy fort, a model butcher's shop, and 'Happy Families' (meet Mr Mug the Milkman and Mr Soot the Sweep). 'Recruiting for Kitchener's Army' looks to be a real scream, with forfeits for defective teeth, smoking, drink and (a hint here of a common reality of childhood among the working-classes) being underdeveloped. Physical drill is the remedy for this offered by the game. A 'Game of Marto' is described on its box as 'jolly', 'amusing', and 'great fun', giving rise to 'laughter' and 'roars'. Snakes and ladders, building bricks and an 'O' gauge railway are all familiar objects.

A collection of metal clockwork toys includes a variety of money boxes, a drummer boy, crawling beetles and a German submarine of about 1939. Boldly illustrated books, such as the *Enid Blyton Books of Fairies*, *The Wonder Book of Ships*, and a book of original nursery rhymes are colourful and magical.

Penny-in-the-slot machines are a feature of Abbey House that conjures up memories of my own childhood in Leeds, of weekend picnics at the Abbey and visits to the museum. In those days you could use the pennies in

Penny-in-the-slot fairground scene

local gritstone. The 'Hark to Rover' Inn contains bar, beer pumps, settle, a pike, Admiral Fitzroy's barometer, and plenty of spittoons. Upstairs is the landlord's parlour, with its picture of Queen Victoria, cases of butterflies and moths – sad and decorative – and another childhood friend – sadder still – the tiger skin rug.

Thomas Sagar's Ironmonger's shop is groaning with goods. So too is Illingworth and Kilburn, Grocers, which has many attractive tins, boxes, jars and other containers. An advertisement for Yorkshire Relish declares it to be 'The most Delicious Sauce in the World'. John Mason, Gentlemen's Hair Cutter, is a super reconstruction with its sinks, chairs, barber's pole, Rossetter's Hair Restorer, shaving brushes, razors and eau de cologne. The price was 4d for a shave, 8d for a haircut, and 6d for Vibrotreatment! Women had to pay 5s 6d for a mud massage.

Castelow's chemist shop and Ann Carter's haberdashery are other shops in the street, but it is the display in the shop of Wilcock & Co. that really

your pocket (if you had any), but now you have to buy the old pennies at the reception desk. Do so, though, if only for the 'Murder in the Museum': if you can work out what is going on, you're cleverer than I am. More obvious are the 'Fairground' and the 'French Guillotine', complete with basket and head. The Auto Stereoscope sets men's pulses racing, but I came off rather predictably in the fortune telling – six daughters, one son, dead at seventy, 'Always Broke'.

Displays of costume, laundry items, lighting, cooking equipment and hearths occupy the Folk galleries. The best of the hearths is an 18th century cast-rion hob grate. A gilded overmantel of around 1820–30, and some 1860s Berlin woolwork face-screens are among other items. Pewter measures, copper kettles, an early pressure cooker (the 'Digester') of 1875, a sausage machine of about 1850, and moulded rolling pins for biscuits give a Victorian feel to the kitchen displays.

Stephen Harding Gate is a reconstructed late-Victorian street, built of

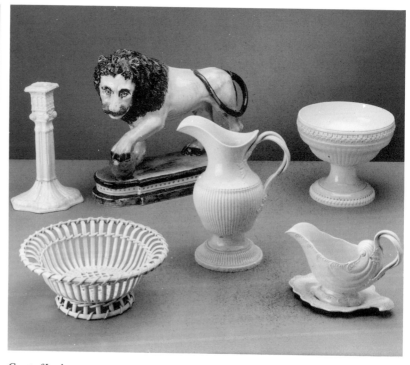

Group of Leeds pottery

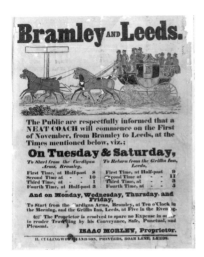

Coach advertisement, 19th century

Leeds City Art Gallery

*Municipal Buildings, The Headrow,
Leeds, West Yorkshire LS1 3AA*
(0532) 462495
Open daily. **F** &
& contact Education Officer
(0532) 462281.

This was the first art gallery I ever visited, as a schoolboy in Leeds, sent there by my teacher to copy a painting. The painting I chose was 'Searchlights' (1916) by Christopher Nevinson, wherein searchlights beam out into the darkness from rooftops. I didn't know it in 1966, but this is an example of the 'Vorticist' abstract art movement in Britain in the early part of this century.

Three paintings by contemporaries of Nevinson can also be associated with the Vorticist movement. 'The Day of Atonement' by Jacob Kramer, an un-usual and powerful *tour-de-force*, is a vision of Jews in prayer shawls. 'The Dance Club (The Jazz Party)' by William Roberts is a wild scene of clubbers dancing, with a strange perspective. 'Praxitella', an extraordinary, cold study of the writer Iris Barry, was painted by the founder of Vorticism, Percy Wyndham Lewis.

Leeds City Art Gallery has an out-standing range of 20th century British art. From the early part of the century, I particularly like 'Lottie of Paradise Walk', a portrait of a flower-seller by William Orpen, based upon a Rem-brandt portrait of his wife as Flora; 'In Sickert's House, Neuville' by Harold Gilman, who became a leading mem-ber of the Camden Town Group, named after the area in London where they lived; 'Portrait of Chloe Boughton-Leigh', a reflective portrait by Gwen John; and 'Lilies' by Matthew Smith, who loved strong, vibrant col-ours. Stanley Spencer is represented by several works in his distinctive and individual style. Biblical scenes were depicted by him as if taking place in his own locality, and 'Christ's Entry into Jerusalem' is just such a religious theme in a modern setting; 'Separating Fighting Swans' has three 'angels' observing a man struggling with swans. 'Hilda, Unity and Dolls' depicts

Stanley Spencer, Hilda, Unity and Dolls,
c.1937

Spencer's first wife and daughter, their eyes contrasting with the black holes of the dolls' eyes.

'Circle of the Monoliths' by Paul Nash, 'The Balcony, Mornington Crescent' by Spencer Gore, 'The Marshalling Yard, Trappes' by Gra-ham Sutherland, and a second painting by Kramer, 'Portrait of Mrs. Philip Pickering', are all works from the first half of this century that are of great interest.

Since the Second World War, Brit-ish art has witnessed many develop-ments, and these can be traced in the rich collections at Leeds. Francis Bacon is arguably the foremost living British painter, and he is represented at Leeds by 'Painting 1950', of a dis-torted figure confined by darkness. Frank Auerbach's 'Maples Demoli-tion, Euston Road' is almost three-dimensional, the paint is applied so thickly. 'Exit the Model' by Bruce McLean depicts figures in blue out-lines, with another outlined in red. I was particularly stuck by 'Monument (Colonial Version)' by Susan Hiller, a rather moving work comprising photo-graphs, a green park bench and an

catches the eye. This is full of Bur-mantofts Pottery, the vibrantly-coloured local art pottery.

Around the corner in Abbey Fold are a clay-pipe maker's, a tobaccon-ist's, a saddler, a wheelwright and join-er, a tin-tack maker, a blacksmith, and a weaver's cottage so typical of the West Riding. Abbey Fold was removed from Hunslet in Leeds, and rebuilt in the museum as found. Through into Harewood Square, and we find clocks and watches, musical instruments, a printer and stationer's, and Leeds pot-tery. All these collections are very good, and the cream Leeds pottery is especially delightful.

Around the walls of the recon-structed street are some interesting notices and signs. Most unusual is the Goldbeater's sign. One poster adver-tises the Bramley and Leeds Coach, another announces Messrs Moritz and Cimex at the Circus, with Miss Saun-ders on the slack wire, and Antipodean Exercises by Master Cannaga. Mr Moritz himself could balance an egg on a straw, and could dance with a peacock's feather on various parts of his body . . . A carousel and a street organ add life to the street scene.

The museum by the Abbey exudes a peculiarly Victorian charm, so that the cares of the real world outside can, for a while, be left behind.

Francis Bacon, Painting 1950

audio-tape. The photographs are of a group of Victorian ceramic plaques in Postman's Park, central London, memorials to people who sacrificed their lives trying to save others. The artist's message is 'Strive to be your own hero'.

Earlier British paintings of note include several by the early-19th-century group of artists based in Norwich, who included John Sell Cotman and John Crome. Constable and Turner are represented by 'Corner of Hampstead Ponds' and a small 'Landscape' respectively. 'Pandora Crowned by the Seasons', by the Victorian painter William Etty, shows Pandora, formed by Vulcan as a statue then brought to life by the gods, being crowned by the four seasons with a garland of flowers.

Another Victorian artist, J. Atkinson Grimshaw, was a local painter of landscapes and townscapes, and Leeds has a number of his works. Among these are 'Autumn Glory (The Old Mill)', an uncannily realistic painting of a brick and stone mill seen through trees. George William Joy was a painter of dramatic historical subjects, none more famous than his 'General Gordon's Last Stand', which portrays Gordon

confronting the hordes of the Mahdi at Khartoum in 1885. 'A Snow Storm' by Edward Scott is of two ponies looking terribly forlorn in the midst of the storm. 'The Red Sofa' by William Mouat Loudan is a portrait of a girl dressed in white on a red sofa. A classic Pre-Raphaelite painting at Leeds is 'The Shadow of Death' by William Holman Hunt, still in the original frame designed by the artist. It shows Mary, mother of Christ, seeing a premonition of His crucifixion in the shadow that He casts on the wall of Joseph's workshop.

Leeds City Art Gallery also has some particularly good French 19th and early 20th century paintings. Jean Corot was a master of understated landscape compositions, and there are two examples in the collection. A later 19th century painter, Gustave Courbet, is represented by 'Les Demoiselles de Village', one of only a handful of works by the artist in British public collections.

Henri Fantin-Latour's 'Portrait of Mme Léon Maitre' is a profile study of the wife of one of his friends by the painter best known for his still life pictures of flowers. 'Les Champs' and 'Soleil Couchant' are two beautiful Impressionist landscapes by Alfred Sisley,

while 'Mother and Child', a thinly-painted oil by Pierre Bonnard, has an informal and immediate charm. 'Barges on the Thames' by André Derain is, by contrast, a riot of violent colour, one of the more famous paintings of the early decades of this century (ill. on cover).

The Gallery is justly renowned for its sculpture, and is the home of the Henry Moore Centre for the Study of Sculpture. Traditional statuary ranges from a marble 'Venus' by Antonio Canova (1757–1822), based on the antique Roman 'Medici Venus', to a bronze of 'The Veiled Venus' (1900) by Ella von Wrede and Kühne Beveridge. 20th century sculpture includes the savage 'Odalisque' by Henri Gaudier-Brzeska, 'Maternity' and 'Baby Asleep' by the controversial Jacob Epstein, and the bronzes 'Forms on a Bow No. 2' and 'AG5' by Eduardo Paolozzi. There are significant works by Henry Moore and Barbara Hepworth, notably 'Maternity' by Moore, and 'Configuration (Phira)', in African guarea wood, by Hepworth.

Four works by younger sculptors are striking in their own ways. 'Delabole Stone Circle' by Richard Long is a circular floor arrangement of delabole slate stone, which doubtless offends

Henry Moore, Reclining Figure, *1929*

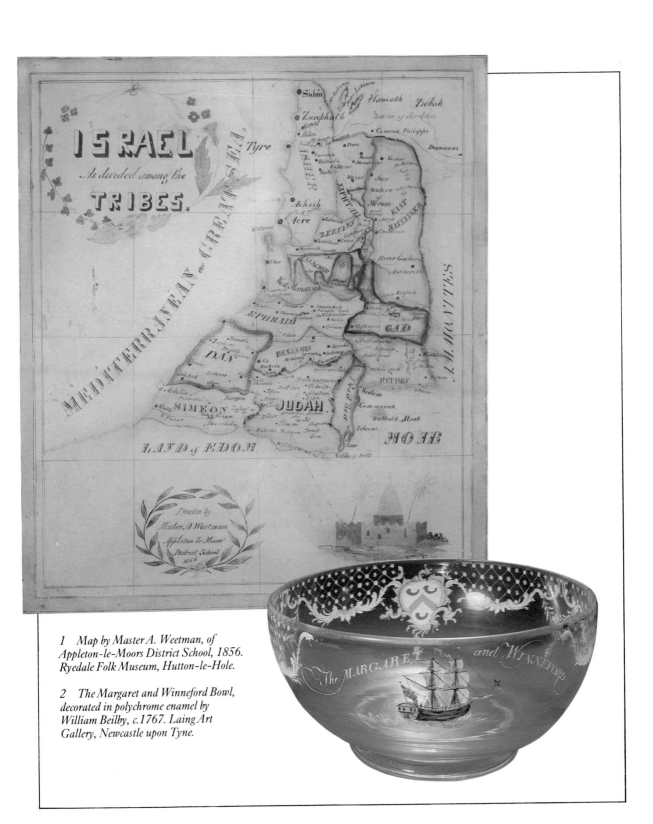

1   Map by Master A. Weetman, of
Appleton-le-Moors District School, 1856.
Ryedale Folk Museum, Hutton-le-Hole.

2   The Margaret and Winneford Bowl,
decorated in polychrome enamel by
William Beilby, c.1767. Laing Art
Gallery, Newcastle upon Tyne.

3   1911 Armstrong Whitworth car.
Museum of Science and Engineering,
Newcastle upon Tyne.

4   *Mummy coffin of Bakt-Hor-Nekht.*
The Hancock Museum, Newcastle upon
Tyne.

5 *opposite*   A Corner of the Artist's
Room, Paris *by Gwen John, c.1907–10.*
Mappin Art Gallery, Sheffield.

6 *top   Le Plongeur by David Hockney,*
1978. Cartwright Hall, Bradford.

7 *above   Replica reconstructing the*
original appearance of the Benty Grange
Helmet. Sheffield City Museum.

8 *right   The Anglo-Saxon Benty Grange*
Helmet, 7th century AD. Sheffield City
Museum.

9 *opposite   A Game of Patience (Miss Margaret Austin-Jones) by Meredith*
Frampton, 1937. Ferens Art Gallery, Hull.

10 *The Blackpool tramcar in the Old Town Street at Beamish. The North of England Open Air Museum, Beamish.*

11 *below Group of Moorcroft pottery. Cannon Hall Museum, Barnsley.*

12 *opposite Still Life with Lobster by Nicolaes van Verendael, 1678. Wakefield Art Gallery.*

13 Whalers in the Arctic *by John Ward, c.1835. Town Docks Museum, Hull.*

14 The Dice Players *by Georges de la Tour, c.1651. Preston Hall Museum, Stockton-on-Tees.*

Jacob Epstein, Maternity, *1910–12*

lovers of more traditional art forms. 'Medicine Wheel' by Chris Drury is a mixed-media sculpture of natural objects arranged in the form of a circular calendar, all the components having some medicinal value. 'Maquette for the Leeds Brick Man' is a lifesize figure made up of fired brick and cement over a fibreglass core, resembling an Egyptian mummy, by Anthony Gormley. This, it is hoped, will lead eventually to the erection somewhere of a 120 feet high version, made of 120,000 bricks.

The fourth of these, and my favourite sculpture, is 'The Cricketer' by Barry Flanagan: a bronze hare jauntily coming in to bowl, perched momentarily atop a set of cricket stumps. Fred Trueman it isn't.

Take all this, add a collection of etchings by Rembrandt, and you have still only touched the surface of the Leeds collections. Go at lunchtime on a Saturday, and you may even be able to dance a foxtrot in the café ...

Lotherton Hall

Aberford, Leeds, West Yorkshire LS25 2EB (0532) 813259
Closed Mondays, except Bank Holidays. 🚻 📷 🅿
 & **S**: steps between levels; **T** in park.
🚻 & 🚻 contact the Keeper.

Lotherton Hall has surprises at every turn. A country house of different periods, it retains an Edwardian feeling of elegance, and some of its best collections date from that period, although 19th century works are also a particular strength.

One of the most important collections is the celebrated one of early Far Eastern ceramics, based on the Frank Savery Bequest, and ranging in date from late Stone Age to the 14th century. A great Neolithic (*c.* 2200–*c.* 1700 BC) Pan-shan-type funerary jar has swirling decoration, and other early pieces are on unglazed red earthenware, some decorated with coloured clays or slips. Han dynasty (206 BC–220 AD) pottery imitations of the expensive ritual bronzes that were used in burials come in a variety of shapes, like birds, dragons and lions. T'ang dynasty (618–906 AD) figures include a vigorous saddle-horse, a poised dancer, and a majestic camel of earthenware with coloured glazes. Among other T'ang period pieces is some exquisite porcelain.

Later, European ceramics range from an 18th century New Hall factory tea service, and Derby, Worcester, Rockingham and Swansea porcelains, to colourful late 19th century Linthorpe and Burmantofts art pottery, and modern Hornsea pottery, as well as 'studio' or individual hand-crafted items. I found some recent pieces by Martin Smith particularly striking: 'Borromini Cloister piece No. 3' (1981) in redware and aluminium, and 'Baroque wall piece No. 2' (1981) in redware, *terra sigillata* slip and slate. There are vases and bottles by Lucy Rie, Hans Coper and Elizabeth Fritsch, and vases by the influential potter and father of 'studio' pottery,

Bernard Leach. Other modern craft works at Lotherton Hall include 'Curve' and 'Quadrangle' neckpieces in acrylic and spray paint by Susanna Heron, David Watkins's 'Russian Orbits' neckpiece in steel wire and neoprene, and a spectacular centre-table and chairs by Fred Baier in stained sycamore.

Sculpture is a particular feature of the Lotherton collections. The earliest pieces are a delightful relief of about 1775 by Thomas Banks, of 'Alcyone discovering the Dead Body of her Husband Ceyx', based on an episode in Ovid's *Metamorphoses*, and a bronze bust of Sir Thomas Gascoigne by Christopher Hewetson (1778), cast by Luigi Valadier. 'A Greek Boxer Waiting his Turn' is an unusual terracotta figure by Joseph Gott of 1828, interesting both for its subject and the study of the male figure. 'The Young Naturalist' by Henry Weekes (1870) is a marble figure of a dreamy and a most unlikely naturalist! 'Liseuse' (The Reader), a 19th century bronze and ivory figure by Albert-Ernest Carrier Belleuse, looked to me for all the world like an Art Deco figure of the 1920s, although not so sinuous.

A number of Dutch and Flemish paintings are on view. The earliest are 'Sea Coast with the Temple of Vesta' by Paul Brill (1554–1626), and 'Adam

Batoni, Sir Thomas Gascoigne, *1779*

A. E. Carrier Belleuse, Liseuse, *before 1887*

and Eve in the Garden of Eden' from the studio of Jan Breughel (1568–1625). The latter is a fantastic scene with lions, an elephant, cheetahs, deer, cattle and other animals, all inhabiting a genuine paradise in harmony, but with the serpent descending the tree

and Eve offering an apple to Adam, who looks unconvinced.

Among the 17th century pictures, 'Dutch Town on a River by Moonlight' is a ghostly landscape by Aert van der Neer, a master of moonlit landscapes. 'Peasants Dancing Outside an Inn' by the Fleming, David Teniers the Younger, depicts peasants dancing to the tune of a piper outside an inn, although no-one looks to be enjoying themselves. One man is slumped over a barrel, another relieves himself in a corner, while a couple fondle each other in the background. Philips Wouwerman's detailed 'Hunting Party' shows hawking on horseback, a woman among the hunters. 'Figures Outside an Inn' by Johannes Lingelbach is an atmospheric painting, the sun glowing through a mist; spot the dog! From the 18th century is 'Picnic in a Park' by Franz Christoph Janneck, a stiff and formal but finely-painted scene, with yet another dog playing a starring role.

A section entitled 'Pets' Corner' has works by the popular 19th century horse-painters J.F. Herring Senior and Junior, and also had some naive Leeds pottery horses when I was there.

Later paintings include many works by the major British Impressionist, Philip Wilson Steer (1860–1942), whose subtle use of colour, and mastery in capturing light and space, are magical to observe. Among 20th century paintings of note are 'An Old Glass Bottle' by William Nicholson, 'Slump' by Edward Wadsworth, and 'Portrait of Dora Morris' by Vanessa Bell.

Lotherton contains quantities of furniture and furnishings. Like the paintings, these are moved around and rearranged from time to time. When I visited, concert pianos by Marsh and Jones dominated one drawing-room, which also boasted a 19th century Chinese screen, a pair of chairs from Windsor Castle, and a lovely marble-topped table of the 1860s, inlaid with birds and fruit, by the architect William Burges, who designed many pieces of furniture. The dining room had a long table by Gillows of about 1810 in mahogany and oak, the New Morning Room a slim barometer of mahogany

and rosewood by John Risso, made around 1805.

A collection of richly styled silver race cups is exhibited together with portraits of the horses that won them, and there are further displays of ornate and striking Victorian silver.

The first floor of the house has more fine pieces of furniture, offering a feast of different types of wood. A table and armchairs by the German architect, Bachen, are of birch and pine, with printed fabric by Liberty, while a corner cabinet by Ernest Gimson of 1903 is made of oak, holly and ebony. A suite of bedroom furniture made by Marsh and Jones in the 1860s for Titus Salt features a half-tester bed and wardrobe in sycamore. Twin beds by Heal & Sons in mahogany with satinwood inlay are complete with the strange Heal patent mattresses. Offering rather a contrast is a papier-maché bedroom suite with mother-of-pearl inlay, characteristic of High Victorian furniture. One of the most interesting pieces is a wardrobe, probably made by Collier and Plucknett of Warwick around 1880, which is of American oak with painted decoration.

Other bits and pieces on display range from a garden table based on a design by Charles Voysey of the 1890s, and a late 18th century garden chair, to a bed cornice of around 1770 by Chip-

The Beverley Race Cup, 1809

Temple Newsam House

Leeds, West Yorkshire LS15 OAE
(0532) 647321
Closed Mondays, except Bank
Holidays. 🚻 🖼 🅿
♿ S: wheelchair access to ground
floor only; T in park.
🎪 & ♟ contact the Keeper.

Painted oak wardrobe by Collier and Plucknett, c.1880

This wonderful country house is basically of 16th and 17th century date, and is set in an extensive park laid out by, among others, the 18th century landscape gardener, Capability Brown. The house was built originally by Thomas, Lord Darcy, later beheaded by Henry VIII. The next owner was the Scottish Earl of Lennox, whose son, Henry, Lord Darnley, born in the house, was to marry Mary Queen of Scots. The son of Darnley and Mary became James VI of Scotland and James I of England, but Darnley himself was murdered in 1567. Mary was beheaded by Elizabeth I in 1587. Afterwards, the house's owners had a less turbulent history.

Today, Temple Newsam is full of decorative and fine art, with particularly good collections of furniture, displayed in some thirty rooms (and frequently rearranged). In addition, much of the internal architecture of the house is itself fascinating.

The first items that I came across of outstanding interest were a bust of the poet and satirist, Alexander Pope by Louis François Roubiliac (1738), and a neoclassical library table made around 1771 by Thomas Chippendale, the great Yorkshire cabinet maker. On the table were displayed ormolu and marble candle vases, and a pedestal clock by Matthew Boulton, also of the 1770s.

The Chinese Drawing Room has gorgeous Chinese decoration of the 1820s, with handpainted wallpaper given by the Prince Regent in 1806. Chinese *famille verte* and *famille rose* porcelain, jades, japanned and decorated lutes, lacquered doors and cupboards, and Chinese-taste Chippendale chairs all combine to show the preferences of Lady Hertford, the room's creator.

At the foot of the late-Victorian oak

pendale, covered in printed cotton in the Chinese taste, and an unfortunate pop-eyed leopard skin. Costumes on show (also changed regularly) included, when I was there, a stylish black crepe 1940s dress with blue, red and yellow flowers, and a blue-and-black printed georgette dress by Alex Grés of 1960. A grotesque beige suede mini-skirt with mink trim by Gucci of

about 1969 left an abiding aftertaste.

Outside the house are extensive gardens, a late 12th century chapel with wall paintings, and a bird garden with hundreds of denizens. Kookaburras, Andean Condors, Marabou Storks, Tawny Eagles, Peach-faced Lovebirds, Occipital Blue Pies, Superb Spreo Starlings, and the Sacred Ibis bring radiant colour to the Elmet landscape.

Stubbs, Phillis, A Pointer, *1772*

staircase is a pedestal organ clock by George Pyke of London (*c.* 1765), with cast ormolu figures representing the Arts and Sciences, said to have been modelled by John Michael Rysbrack. The clock is supposed to have belonged to Marie Antoinette.

A winking devil in a marble chimneypiece welcomes us to the first floor in the West Wing, where a series of paintings decorates the walls of several chambers. The best of these, unusually, are by British artists. Prominent are 'Phillis, A Pointer of Lord Clermont's' by the great 18th century animal painter and anatomist George Stubbs, and the 'Portrait of Elizabeth Prowse' by Thomas Gainsborough, whose stunning and fluid portraits epitomise the relaxed yet lively spirit of the second half of the 18th century. A contemporary of Gainsborough's, Joseph Wright of Derby, is better known for his scenes from contemporary life that employ striking use of light and shadow, but he was also a skilled portraitist, as can be seen from his 'Portrait of a Girl in a Red Dress'. Somewhat earlier is the 'Portrait of Miss Ingram' from the studio of Sir Peter Lely, a Dutchman who became England's most influential portrait painter in the 17th century. There are landscapes in addition to the portraits, and 'San Georgio Maggiore' by Francesco Guardi, 'Coastal Scene with Fishermen' in the style of Claude-Joseph Vernet, and 'Italianate Landscape' by Richard Wilson are three 18th century landscapes that stand out.

The first floor rooms in the West Wing also house the only complete

Henry Morland, The Fair Nun Unmasked, *late 18th century*

Chelsea tea and coffee service in existence, of around 1758–60 in date, decorated with views of architectural remains. Derby figures, Bow candlesticks, 18th century Dutch delftware plaques, oriental blue and white porcelain, and three delightful 18th century Spanish tin-glazed earthenware plaques (representing *Amours Pastorales,* Christ Disputing with the Doctors, and Allegory of Earth) show the range of Temple Newsam's ceramic collections. Also worthy of close study are a set of chairs by Giles Grendey (*c.* 1735–40)

in beech, japanned scarlet and gold, with cane seats; a bronze 'Lion Attacking a Horse' by or after the masterful Italian sculptor Giambologna (1524–1608); and two marvellous wall brackets bearing 18th century Italian cats in carved, gilded and painted wood.

The sizeable Saloon contains European paintings, and a remarkable set of twenty chairs, four settees and a daybed with their original English needlework upholstery of 1746. Best of the paintings are the energetic 'Still Life of Flowers and Fruit' by the distinguished

Slipware charger by Thomas Toft, 1674

A twenty-four-inch diameter slip-ware dish of 1674 by the potter Thomas Toft is a typically vivacious example of these unsophisticated wares, and leads visitors on to the upper floor of the South Wing of this rambling old house. There is furniture in abundance here, with mirrors, carpets and sculptures, memorable among which is a dwarf bookcase of mahogany, oak and pine, painted with green chinoiserie, by Thomas Chippendale.

Two of the loveliest paintings in the house are in this wing: the 'Portrait of Isabella Anne Ingram' by the great 18th century portraitist, Sir Joshua Reynolds, and 'The Fair Nun Unmasked' by Henry Morland, also of the 18th century and interesting for its portrayal of a woman in fancy dress as worn at a masque, with her lowered mask in her hand. Among decorative art here are a group of Longton Hall ceramic figures of about 1759, representing Africa, Europe, Asia and America, and a spectacular Javanese chair of Chinese rosewood, carved around 1760. There is also a small marble 'Bust of a Negro Boy' of the 17th century Italian School.

In the Darnley Room hang a number of 17th century Dutch and Flemish paintings. These include 'Interior of the Cathedral, Antwerp' (1653) by Pieter Neefs the Younger, 'Storm off Egmond Van Zee' by Jacob van Ruis-

Dutch artist, Rachel Ruysch (1664–1750); 'Landscape with Cottage' (1661) by Cornelis van Swieten; and a pretty 16th century Flemish School 'Adam and Eve', with rabbits symbolising lust. An imposing portrait of a former owner of the house, Sir Arthur Ingram, painted by George Geldorp in 1642, is the essence of a wealthy country gentleman of that period. The fame of Italian 16th century Giorgio Vasari rests on his biographies of Italian artists from Cimabue to Titian, but he was also a painter himself, and his 'Temptation of St. Jerome' can be seen here. In the Library off the Saloon are two terrestrial and celestial globes of about 1760–70 by John Bennett.

dael, and an exquisite oil painting on copper, 'Landscape with Sportsmen and Dogs' by Paul Brill. Nearby is a primitive painting by Sebastian Vranx entitled 'The Death of Gerard Leckerbeetje', showing dubious fighting methods adopted during the Dutch War of Independence, consisting largely of cavalry firing guns at each other at point-blank range!

Part of the Kirkleatham Centrepiece

The Nursery features a beautiful early-18th-century Indian looking glass, the frame of rosewood inlaid with pearlshell, ivory and brass. The same room has a marvellous carved lime picture frame of about 1685, framing a portrait of the first Earl of Craven. Better still are a sofa and daybed, among the most important in the country because of the unique survival of their original cut-velvet Genoa silk upholstery.

There is much more to see at Temple Newsam – Tudor and Stuart oak furniture; busts by Joseph Gott; Gillows furniture; mirrors; wall lights; sparkling pink-tinted Venetian glass; silver (especially the Kirkleatham Centrepiece of 1731–32); 19th century metalware; even Peruvian furniture. The house is one of the real art treasure troves of the region, and a must for any visitor to the area. I've forgiven my old economics and cross-country master, Mr Clegg, for making me run round Temple Newsam park on all those awful wintry Wednesday afternoons!

Writing table commissioned for the Georgian Library at Temple Newsam, c.1745

MIDDLESBROUGH

Captain Cook Birthplace Museum

Stewart Park, Middlesbrough, Cleveland   (0642) 311211
Closed Mondays. 🏛️📷🅿️ ♿W
🚻 & 👫 contact Curator at Dorman Museum (0642) 813781.

Britain's most famous explorer was born in 1729 in Marton, now part of Middlesbrough, the second son of eight children, to a farm labourer. From these humble beginnings Cook went on to claim Australia and New Zealand for the British monarchy, and discovered and charted numerous Pacific Islands before being killed in 1779 by natives in Hawaii. This museum stands as a tribute to Cook, and marks the start of the Captain Cook Heritage Trail in Cleveland and North Yorkshire (details of which are obtainable from the museum or local tourist offices).

In the course of his adventurous life Cook worked as a shop assistant in Staithes, and as an apprentice on a collier ship sailing out of **Whitby**, before joining the Royal Navy as an able seaman in 1755. The museum has displays relating to his early life, and to life at sea. In a reconstruction of below-decks on board one of Cook's ships, HM Barque 'Endeavour', there are examples of sailors' crafts like scrimshaw, an iron tobacco box of 1791 with a view of Tahiti, a carved bamboo tobacco jar, and a rare 18th century hand-made fishing line and implement.

In the 18th century, sailors determined their latitude (distance north or south of the equator) by observing the sun with a quadrant. Shortly before Cook's first voyage the *Nautical Almanac* was published, enabling sailors to calculate longitude (distance east or west of Greenwich). Cook took with him for navigation on his first Pacific voyage a theodolite, an azimuth compass, an astronomical quadrant and a

Early carved Maori figure

sextant. On display are a sextant, an octant and a compass, all very grand.

In the same gallery is a detailed model of Cook's ship, the 'Endeavour'. Originally built in Whitby in 1764 as a collier ship of a type known as 'cats',

she was at first called the 'Earl of Pembroke'. The ship was bought by the Royal Navy in 1768 for £2,480. 10s 11d; she was 106 ft long, weighed 366 tons, and carried a crew of about 100. There are two more fine ship models in the museum by the same builder, a Captain Lawrence, of the 'Yosemite', a three-masted barque built in 1768, and the 'Derwent', another three-masted ship which was built in 1784.

The first of Cook's three great voyages of discovery (1768–71) took him round Cape Horn to Tahiti, New Zealand and Australia. The purpose of the voyage was primarily to make astronomical observations from Tahiti, but also to search for the 'Southern continent' that was known of but had never been explored. Although Australia had first been sighted by a European in 1606, it was Cook who discovered and charted the eastern seaboard in 1770. His second voyage (1772–75) took him around the Cape of Good Hope in HMS 'Resolution', another Whitby 'cat', and further south than anybody had ever been in search of the Antarctic. His third voyage (1776–80) was made in order to search for a western

Display of wallabies

entry to the North-West passage around the northern coast of Canada. En route he visited Tasmania, New Zealand (for the fifth time), Christmas Island, and Hawaii, before returning from the Bering Sea to meet his death in Hawaii.

The museum has collections from places visited by Cook, notably Canada, Australia and New Zealand. The Canadian material is dominated by a totem pole sited outside the museum, which was presented by the Government and people of Vancouver Island in recognition of Cook's visit there in 1778, on his third voyage (ill. on cover). The design of the pole is based on two traditional carvings of the Nootka Indians of Vancouver. One of these is the mythical Thunderbird, hunter of whales, which caused thunder and lightning; the other is the Bear Crest, which appears on a pole in the abandoned village of Ehatisaht, said to have belonged to the wife of Old Captain Jack, a descendant of Callicum, a chief who met Cook.

Other Canadian items in the museum include a war bonnet, moccasins, a dance mask from Nootka Sound, a necklet, a frog dish, rattles, basketwork, paddles, a wicker baby carrier, a box made of porcupine quills, a snow sledge, and a traditional fur trapper's outfit. All these are watched over by a Polar Bear and a Grizzly Bear.

Australian Aboriginal culture is one of the wonders of the modern world. The tragedy of the suppression of the native Australians by the white nations is one of the most shameful chapters in modern history. Despite this, we are still able to discern the remarkable traditional ways of life of the Aborigines, both in their surviving culture, particularly in North Australia, and through their material culture – their art and artefacts. The Captain Cook Museum shows aspects of the life of these hunter-gatherers, encountered by Cook at Botany Bay in 1770. On display are bracelets of bird feathers, clapping sticks, *digeridus* (musical instruments that make a droning sound), a hat worn during the *corroboree* ceremony, bark painting, and a mysterious

Dance drum from the Solomon Islands

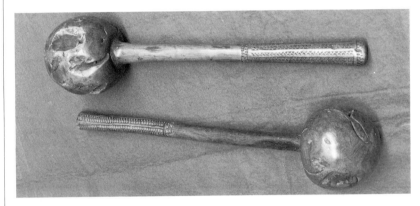

Clubs said to be those used to kill Captain Cook

small funerary totem pole. There are also shields, boomerangs, war clubs, a barbed spear, a stone axe (the Aborigines had no iron until the Europeans came), and fire sticks. Aborigine music swirls around a gallery also inhabited by wallabies, a dingo, koala bears and, of course, a duck-billed platypus. We have become so used to these strange words and sights through television that we often forget what a unique country Australia is. For Cook and his men the amazement was undiminished.

New Zealand is represented by Maori artefacts, such as carved figures, a carved Maori face, a flax shirt, ceremonial staffs, a *wakahuia* or treasure box to store prized feathers, a cosmetics box, model canoes, and hand clubs of whalebone, wood and greenstone. There is a greenstone *tiki*, a human image representing an ancestor, with large head and thrust-out tongue. *Tiki* images are common throughout Maori art.

More Pacific material – a dance drum, clubs, axes, maces, fans, a fly whisk, bamboo combs – come from Fiji, New Caledonia, the Gilbert Islands, the Solomon Islands, and other island groups visited by Cook. Of curiosity value are a piece of the rock on which Cook is supposed to have fallen when struck by a priest at Kealakekua Bay in Hawaii, and the two clubs said to have been the actual ones used to kill him. This was a sad end for a man whose great spirit drove him to write in the log of HMS 'Resolution' on 30th January 1774: 'I had Ambition not only to go farther than anyone had done before, but as far as it was possible for any man to go.'

The museum has a conservatory, which houses thousands of exotic plants from all over the world, the eastern section contains many plants native to Australia and the Pacific Islands. The whole is set in the attractive Stewart Park, which has an aviary and a small zoo.

Dorman Museum

*Linthorpe Road, Middlesbrough,
Cleveland   (0642) 813781*
Closed Sundays and Mondays. ⓕ
ⓟ
♿ ST: wheelchair access to
ground floor only.
🏛 & 🚻 contact Curator/Assistant
Curator.

Middlesbrough is a most unusual town
in that prior to 1830 it was no more
than a lonely farm. A true child of the
Industrial Revolution, it was created
when the Middlesbrough Pottery was
started here in 1834. Within thirty
years the town's population had grown
to about 20,000. Despite the fact that
there were several museums established in this region long before the
town was thought of, Middlesbrough's
Dorman Museum has some old and
important collections.

Probably the best of those on show is
the extraordinary Nelson Collection of
birds, birds' eggs and birds' nests,
presented to the town in 1918 by Mrs
T.H. Nelson. These were put on display in 1924, and have remained there
ever since. There are hundreds of local
birds, all displayed in reconstructed
habitats, ranging in size from the
Whooper Swan to long-tail tits, marsh
tits, and cole tits. There are thousands
of eggs of all kinds, with an especially
large collection of several hundred
guillemot eggs, mostly collected in the
1880s and 1890s, long before it became illegal to do so, as it is today.

In the same Nelson Room is displayed a collection of shells, which fully
deserves close attention. Shells are the
hard parts of molluscs or brachiopods,
and are needed to support and protect
the soft bodies of those creatures. The
shells are made mostly of calcium car-
bonate, and grow with the animal.
While there are only 250 species of
brachiopod left in the world, there are
over 100,000 species of mollusc.
There are six classes of mollusc, including Gastropoda (80,000 species),
Bivalvia (20,000 species), Monopla-
cophora, and Cephalopoda. Monopla-
cophora were believed to have been

Linthorpe Pottery vase

extinct for 350 million years until
specimens were dredged up from very
deep water in 1952. Cephalopoda include cuttlefish, squid and octopus.

There really are some lovely shells
here, with a great variety of shapes,
patterns and colours – pinks, blues,
browns, greys, yellows and greens.
Among the most attractive are shells of

Nautilus pompilius (ill. on cover), *Murex
scalopax* (spiny), *Haliotis iris* (pearly interior), cowry shells (glossy and patterned), and the shell of *Pecten maximus*
(pink, the classic scallop shape).

Natural history continues in the
museum's aquarium, which also has a
huge fossil *Ichthyosaurus* head, and a
working model of a local landmark, the
Transporter Bridge of 1911. More fossils, including vertebrae from the said
Ichthyosaurus, are in the Geology gallery. One of these is the massive fossil
tooth of the Carcharodon shark, a
monster of the Miocene period (25
million years ago) which grew up to
fifty feet long – twice the size of the
biggest modern Great White Sharks.
Carcharodon's jaws were six foot wide,
tooth to tooth, when open – a fearsome
creature indeed.

The Making of Middlesbrough gallery ranges over all sorts of subjects. It
begins with the founding in 1834 of the
Middlesbrough Pottery, which specialised in strictly functional wares, such as
bowls, plates, wash-basins and jugs,
much of them for export, before it
closed in 1887. More renowned was
the Linthorpe Pottery, founded in
1879 as the Middlesbrough Art Pottery. Using local red brick clay, and
later imported white clay, the Pottery
became famous for its rich glazes and
unusual forms. Its specialist output was
artistic vases and bowls, but it also
produced marmalade jars, sardine
dishes ink bottles, ash trays, umbrella
and parasol handles, clock cases, gong
frames, dados, finger plates, card trays
and lots more. The Pottery had a sadly
short life, its owner's involvement in
1889 in a Building Society collapse
leading to the Pottery's closure in
1890. There are many fine examples of
Linthorpe pottery in the Dorman.

Another major local industry was
iron and steel manufacture, based on
local ironstone mining, coal, and water
transport. The first foundry was that of
H.F. Bolckow, who in 1840 set up a
brass and iron foundry to make
anchors, chain, cable and rail, steam
engines and wagons. A flavour of the
industry is provided by mining tools
and lamps, and tools and novelty pieces
of iron manufacture.

Cradle in the shape of a boat

ments and wit can be found (I only wish I knew). The other is a post-mortem set, with the appropriate blades and saws . . . .

Two more items stand out in particular: a cradle in the shape of a boat named 'Lilian'; and a watercolour of Middlesbrough in 1858, when it was still less than thirty years old, by Joseph Blossom. The painting shows a two-masted brig of the type that used to transport coal from the North East to London, a steam tug, and people fishing in the Tees for salmon.

Finally, who could resist the invitation issued by the Oddfellows Hall in January 1884 to see Mr Nicholas Morgan, the great phrenologist and mesmerist, and Mr John Matthews who, while mesmerised *and* blindfolded, would read music and play the flute? Mesmerism certainly ain't what it was.

A section on Health contains two unusual exhibits. One is a phrenologist's head (phrenology is the so-called science of mental faculties located in various parts of the skull), which shows where hope, firmness, moral senti-

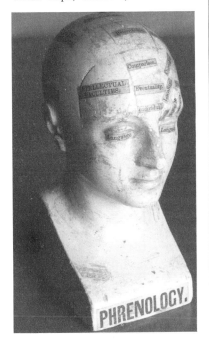

Phrenologist's head

Joseph Blossom, Middlesbro' 1858

NEWCASTLE UPON TYNE

The Greek Museum

The University, Newcastle upon Tyne,
Tyne and Wear NE1 7RU
(091) 232 8511
Closed Saturdays and Sundays.
F   **&W**
♿ & **♞** must be booked in
advance, maximum 15 people:
contact the Curator or the Classics
Department secretary.

Just 100 yards from the better-known
Museum of Antiquities is another of
Newcastle University's museums. The
Greek Museum occupies only a single
small room, but has important collections of Ancient Greek material that
deserve a wider audience.

This tiny and unexpected treasure-
house has Bronze Age items from
Mycenae, and later items from all over
the Ancient Greek world. The Mycenean section has a graceful stemmed
cup of 1300–1200 BC. Among the
later pottery there is a series of
perfumed-oil containers in different
shapes, such as those of a siren, a
bivalve shell, a swan, a female bust, a
crouching dwarf and, best of all, a
duck, the last probably Corinthian of
about 600 BC.

Animal and human representations
abound in Greek art, and here you can

Mycenean kylix

Greek volute krater with a Dionysiac scene, 450–425 BC

see a Gorgon, gods and goddesses,
battle scenes, wild boar, horses, bulls,
even a tortoise, all in bronze, stone or
pottery, or decorating vases and other
vessels. There is a superb large vase, or
Volute Krater, of 450–425 BC, showing a Dionysiac scene featuring the

ritual dismemberment of a wild animal.

Armour, like all dress, is a particularly compelling link with the past, and
the Greek Museum has two magnificent bronze helmets, which immediately remind us of the warlike
nature of Ancient Greek society that

Corinthian oil container

Corinthian helmet

accompanied its stupendous artistic and intellectual achievements. One is late 7th century BC, of the Corinthian type, with close-fitting skull shape, nose guard, and small openings for eyes and mouth; it is the very image of the Greek hoplite warrior. The other helmet is Illyrian, of the late 6th century BC, also close-fitting but with an open face. The museum also has a carefully modelled bronze leg-guard of the early 5th century BC, and a rare bronze spearbutt, the 'blunt' end of a spear, which allowed the weapon to be planted in the ground. This is probably Macedonian, of the late 4th century BC, that is the period of Alexander the Great.

Along with the **Museum of Antiquities**, the Greek Museum provides a dramatic insight into the two great classical civilisations, whose power and influence still surge across the centuries.

The Hancock Museum

The University, Newcastle upon Tyne, Tyne and Wear NE2 4PT
(091) 222 7418/232 2359
Open daily. 🅴🅿
& S: wheelchair access to most of ground floor, but none to first floor.
🚹 & 🚻 book in advance: phone (091) 222 6753. ☺

What do Egyptian mummies, snowy owls, Thomas Bewick and meteorites have in common? Answer – you can find them all in the magnificent Hancock Museum in Newcastle. A museum of natural history first and foremost, the Hancock houses tremendous collections, particularly of birds, but with very important ethnography too (the latter would have been even more important if the University hadn't sold the spectacular George Brown collection to the Japanese in 1985).

Everything you ever wanted to know about birds is here at the Hancock, all related in a friendly, accessible way: habitat, adaptation, courtship, eggs, migration, feeding, evolution, flight, birdwatching, conservation, and lots more.

Did you know that the peregrine can fly at 180 mph (a swift reaches 60 mph)? Or that carrier pigeons relayed news of the conquest of Gaul to Rome, and news of the Battle of Waterloo to London? Or that canaries are fifteen times more sensitive to gas than humans, hence their use as warning devices in mines? Or that Falconry originated in Arabia? Or that the egg of the extinct Elephant Bird, *Aepyornis*, could hold two gallons and is the largest known single cell in the animal kingdom?

Birds have fascinated humans for centuries, endowed as they are with the magical gift of flight, and myths, legends and folklore surround many species. In ancient Egypt the heron was the soul of Ra, the sun god; later its fat became a cure for rheumatism; in the Faroe Islands a heron's foot is carried to ensure fishing success. The Romans believed goose fat to be an aphrodisiac (is there *anything* in the world that hasn't been tried?), while eating a goose at Christmas is probably a much older pre-Christian tradition. To hear the first cuckoo of spring is lucky, and by counting its calls girls could discover how many years they would remain unwed.

Some birds are associated with death and disaster. Ill-treat a robin and you court bad luck, while it is a bad omen if it enters a house or a mine. The albatross brings bad weather if it flies around a ship, and it too must not be ill-treated, or else. Owls are surrounded by mystery, with their strange eyes and nocturnal shrieks and hoots. They were once thought to drink the blood of infants, and to appear when death was near (the brew of Macbeth's witches included an owlet's wing . . .). Nevertheless owls have been hung up in the country to avert storms and other disasters, and the Romans used them to combat the evil eye; both Athene (Greek goddess of wisdom) and Merlin are associated with owls.

Snowy Owl

Not much good, though, can be said of ravens, which have been seen as heralds of death (in *Macbeth* a raven croaks the fatal entrance of Duncan), and as the ghosts of murdered folk, the steeds of witches, as well as the messengers of the sun god, Phoebus. The wren-hunt is descended from a pagan ritual, and originated as a sacrifice at the winter solstice to defeat dark powers and ensure the coming of spring; the wren is traditionally hunted on St Stephen's Day, as it was a wren that awoke St Stephen's gaolers when he was trying to escape prison.

Birds in danger is a horribly recurrent theme at the Hancock, and danger presents itself in many guises, most of them directly attributable to humans. Most obviously there is the hunting of birds for 'sport'. Shooting birds started seriously with the development of the shotgun, and one of the most obscene of all records is the 2,929 grouse slaughtered in a single day with eight guns (that's about 365 dead grouse per sportsman in the day). Humans have

caged birds, such as buderigars, mynahs and parrots (and killed many in transit from their homelands); set them upon each other so as to gamble, as in cockfighting (which is recorded as far back as the 5th Century BC); and killed them for their plumage, and to build egg collections. We have persecuted birds for no good reason: the sea eagle, the red kite, the hen harrier, the merlin have all been hunted and trapped. We hit them with our aeroplanes, we kill 2½ million a year on our roads (most of them – over one million – sparrows), and we cake them in oil from accidents (the Torrey Canyon wreck killed at least 10,000 birds) and from the illegal jettisoning of oil from tankers. Worst of all, we poison them or their food by using toxic chemicals on farms, and by discharging toxic industrial waste. We also clear forests and drain marshland, thus destroying scarce habitats.

Humans have managed to kill off about 130 species of birds since we exterminated the dodo in 1690, among

them the heath hen (extinct 1932), the pink-headed duck (extinct 1944), and what was once probably the world's most common bird, the passenger pigeon (extinct 1914). The Hancock has the only specimen in the world of a young Great Auk (extinct 1852).

The greatest strength of the Hancock is its birds, but the rest of the animal kingdom is also on show, whether dead or alive. Mammals are displayed in Abel's Ark, a light-hearted way to put as many animals on view as possible – bison, polar bear, tiger, wolf, wombat, cobra, lion, moose, rhinoceros, even mole and rat rowing a boat!

Invertebrates, too, are here in very large numbers, with butterflies, moths, ants, bees, beetles (some as big as a child's hand) all jostling for space. The microscopic world is also on view. Read all the captions, and you may never drink or eat (or get out of bed, or into it!) again.

Volcanoes, earthquakes, swamps, deserts, mountains, the Ice Age, the planets, fossils, rocks and minerals make up the Geology gallery, which begins 'About three minutes and ten seconds after our Universe began, helium molecules formed', and continues with a cake to mark the 4,600,000th birthday of the Solar System. Once again, accessible messages and a huge amount to see.

The ethnography collections are also of the highest quality. They range from ancient Egypt, with two mummies, one in full view, the other mercifully still in her coffin (colour plate 4), to more modern North American material. There is a great variety of shoes, hats, head-dresses, masks, weapons, bags and jewellery, many of the most fantastic designs. Outstanding among all these treasures are the Japanese armour, a Sri Lankan ceremonial dancing mask, and a New Hebridean figure commemorating the man whose skull is set upon it. Among my favourite exhibits here are a Chinese medicine box full of the most unlikely substances, and a splendid smoking-cap from Arabia. These items give us the merest of glimpses into rich foreign cultures, and in many ways are com-

Display of animals in Abel's Ark

Sacred crown of a Yoruba king

Group of hats from the Hancock Museum's collections

pletely unrepresentative; but they are the most marvellous stimulus to the imagination.

As if all this wasn't enough, the Hancock has a 'shrine' to Thomas Bewick (1753–1828), the famous Newcastle wood engraver, whose work has been used to illustrate thousands of books. Bewick was a naturalist, and while his commercial work consisted of letterheads, banknotes and so on, he produced two volumes of engravings on British birds and one on 'Quadrupeds'. The Hancock has a large collection of his drawings and engravings.

The Hancock Museum can be quite exhausting, but may well be the best museum of its type in combining extensive collections with a friendly way of displaying them. An abiding memory is the eight-foot tall green dragon that sits in the entrance . . . a Bobby Dazzler of a museum, this.

Laing Art Gallery

Higham Place, Newcastle upon Tyne, Tyne and Wear NE1 8AG
(091) 232 6989
Closed Mondays. ♿ **W**: entrance for disabled at side; lift to upstairs gallery.
🍴 & 👥 welcome, book in advance if talk or tour required; small groups can visit stores by prior arrangement. ☼

Anyone who harbours illusions about the North East being populated by dour and philistine Geordies should visit the Laing Art Gallery to see that culture and the arts flourish in this great city. Built for £30,000 in 1901–4 by local wine and spirit merchant Alexander Laing, the Laing Art Gallery houses collections of fine and decorative art that have been built up largely thanks to a long series of gifts and bequests.

For over 450 years, Newcastle had its own assay office, and the Laing Art Gallery's silver collection is impressive, with a sizeable number of early pieces from the 16th and 17th centuries. These include the Sawley Flagon, made by William Ramsay around 1670 and presented to the Mayor Of Newcastle. Eventually, it ended up in Sawley parish church, in the West Riding of Yorkshire, which sold it to the Laing in 1952. Equally fine are three silver-gilt standing cups and covers of the Merchant Adventurers of Newcastle, dated 1649.

Glassmaking started on Tyneside in 1619. The Laing's collection includes many examples of local manufacture – wine glasses, mead glasses, cordial glasses, ale glasses, cider glasses, jelly glasses, decanters, flasks, a loving cup, rummers, candlesticks, and a lacemaker's lamp. There isn't, in truth, much that cannot be made in glass, and the Laing even has a glass sword! The most beautiful items are the glasses with air twist and opaque twist stems, dating from the mid-18th century onwards. Pressed glass may not be quite so appealing, but its manufacture brought glass within the price range of

Claret decanter enamelled by William Beilby,
c.1770

a wide group of people, and into the age of mass-production.

Legend has it that the rise of the pottery manufacturer, C.T. Maling & Sons Ltd, began when Christopher Maling sold a case of jam-jars to two old ladies in Dundee. The ladies turned out to be the Keiller sisters, whose marmalade became world famous. Having begun in Sunderland in 1762, the Maling business moved to Newcastle and endured for 200 years, producing a variety of pottery, including some classic designs of the 1920s and '30s. The Laing's ceramic collections include local wares such as these, but also range in time and style from a 5th century BC Athenian storage jar to some horrible Spanish jugs of the 1940s.

Costumes on display in museums have to be changed frequently because textiles soon deteriorate when exposed to light and air. Thus, like elsewhere, only a small proportion of the Laing's collections can be seen at any one time. On my most recent visit there was a display entitled 'La Belle Epoque 1890–1914', consisting of day, afternoon and evening dresses, with hats and shoes. Not my favourite period for costume – the women's styles often look dowdy compared with the exuberance of the 1920s – but all costume is intriguing in that it evokes a sense of time more immediately than, perhaps, any other type of object.

Two exhibits are of outstanding interest among the other decorative art collections: the 19th century Japanese *Norimono* or sedan chair, made from lacquered wood and used as transport by high-ranking samurai and merchants; and the two stained glass windows commissioned in 1896 for St Cuthbert's church, Newcastle, illustrating scenes from the Second Book of Samuel. The latter were designed by Edward Burne-Jones in the Pre-Raphaelite style, and dominate the gallery in which they are displayed.

The painting collections are strong in local works. Alfred Dixon's oil, 'Get Up', based upon pitman Joseph Skipsey's poem, portrays a miner going to work in the small hours, kissing his sleeping child, watched by his wife (who, remarkably, resembles a Greek goddess): '"Get up!" the caller calls, "Get up!" / And in the dead of night, / To win the bairns their bite and sup, / I rise a weary wight. // My flannel dudden donn'd, thrice o'er / My birds are kiss'd, and then / I with a whistle shut the door / I may not ope again.'

Other evocative local views include George Horton's 'Mouth of the Tyne', and 'Morpeth Bridge' by that supreme 18th century watercolourist, Thomas Girtin.

The Laing has many Victorian oil paintings – so popular nowadays, yet once so derided – with a number of good later works, and a few earlier ones. Among the earlier pictures are 'Peasant Ploughing with Two Horses' by Thomas Gainsborough, an early work by the 18th century master of portraiture, and two 18th century scenes from everyday life by George Morland, 'Evening or The Post Boy's Return' and 'Paying the Ostler'. The gallery also has two paintings by John Constable, 'Yarmouth Jetty' and 'Flatford Lock on the Stour' (although the latter does not rival his better-known Flatford Mill series). There is a rarity too – a painting by the renowned 18th century Italian townscape painter, Antonio Canaletto 'Prato della Valle, Padua' with no water in sight!

The striking paintings by local artist John Martin (1789–1854) are hardly to

Thomas Girtin, Morpeth Bridge, *c.1802*

John Martin, The Bard, *exhibited 1817*

on a German legend of a wandering knight who visits Venusberg and abandons himself to a life of sensual pleasure. Other notable paintings of the 19th century are 'The Catapult', a Roman re-creation by Edward Poynter, the bustling 'Stagshaw Bank Fair' by John Ritchie, and 'Alfred, the Saxon

Holman Hunt, Isabella and the Pot of Basil, *1866–68*

Clausen, The Stone Pickers, *1887*

everybody's taste with their grandiose treatment of dramatic or apocalyptic stories, but I love them. The Laing Art Gallery has several of his works, of which 'The Bard' is a good example of his style, wherein the last surviving Welsh Bard hurls curses at the host of Edward I from atop a crag, before throwing himself into the torrent below. This actually made me laugh, and

not many paintings do that! As for 'The Destruction of Sodom and Gomorrah', you'll just have to see for yourself.

Two major Pre-Raphaelite paintings – 'Isabella and the Pot of Basil' by William Holman Hunt and 'Laus Veneris' by Edward Burne-Jones – are based on poems, the first on one by Keats wherein Isabella's lover is murdered by her brothers, and the second

King in the Camp of Guthrum the Dane', an exotic historical fantasy by Daniel Maclise.

20th century paintings and sculpture offer a rich and varied selection. You will find sculpture as diverse as Albert Toft's erotic 'The Spirit of Contemplation' and Henry Moore's 'Seated Woman (Thin Neck)', and paintings ranging from Walter Sickert's impressionistic 'Piazza San Marco' to Stanley Spencer's realistic yet dream-like 'The Lovers, or The Dustman', and Duncan Grant's richly coloured 'Provençal Landscape' to L.S. Lowry's 'Old Chapel, Newcastle upon Tyne' in drab tones. Contemporary works are now being acquired, beginning with 'Germania' by R.B. Kitaj. My particular favourite among the paintings is Laura Knight's 'The Beach', which encapsulates the endless sun-filled summer of seaside childhood.

In addition to oil paintings, there are also many watercolours, likewise by famous and lesser-known artists from the 18th to 20th centuries. There were good British works on show when I was there, including 'St Paul's in November' by George Clausen and 'Norway 1940' by Eric Ravilious. Watercolour displays are changed regularly throughout the year.

The Laing is an art gallery that is always full of interest, and undoubtedly houses one of the best collections of paintings in the North.

Harold Knight, At the Piano, *c.1921*

Museum of Antiquities

The University, Newcastle upon Tyne, Tyne and Wear NE1 7RU
(091) 232 8511 ext. 7844/7849
Closed Sundays. ▣ ♿
♿ & ♿ advance booking preferred; guided tours on prior request.

This museum has the best Roman collections that have been put together in the vicinity of that most extraordinary of Roman remains in Britain, Hadrian's Wall. The collections were begun in 1813 by the newly-founded Society of Antiquaries of Newcastle upon Tyne, and both the Society and the collections continue to flourish over 170 years later. Together with those of the nearby **Greek Museum**, also on the Newcastle University campus, the collections of the Museum of Antiquities are a minor revelation.

A tiny harpoon made from deerhorn, of about 6000 BC, is one of the oldest artefacts ever found in the North East. It is accompanied by other Stone Age material from the Newcastle region, notably a collection of vessels known as 'beakers', the makers of which have been termed the 'Beaker People'. In about 2000 BC these Neolithic (late-Stone-Age) people migrated from the Iberian Peninsula, and some settled in the British Isles. They created this distinctive form of pottery, which was normally deposited with their dead. A more familiar legacy are the circles of standing stones that they erected all over the country, of which the most famous is the early phase of Stonehenge.

The Bronze Age is very well represented in the museum, with earthenware food vessels and bronze weapons. Among these collections is the Wallington Hoard, consisting mostly of axeheads and spearheads, all from the 8th century BC. Slightly later (*c.* 600 BC) is the Whittingham hoard of swords and spearheads, which were found set in a circle and standing upright in peat. This hoard is in beautiful condition.

Another marvellous Bronze-Age piece is a bronze shield found at Tribley, two feet in diameter, and originally

The Tribley Shield, Bronze Age

backed with wood and leather. Apparently, its early-19th-century finder decided to cut it into pieces to give to his friends, so it has undergone extensive restoration! It probably had a ceremonial rather than defensive purpose.

The real strength of the collection is the Roman material, and in particular a unique series of inscribed and sculptured stones, which are valuable evidence of life on Hadrian's Wall.

The most significant of these is the group of Mithraic altars, and 'The Birth of Mithras' pierced relief. These come from Mithraic temples at Rudchester, Carrawburgh and Housesteads. Mithras was a god of Persian and Zoroastrian origin, who exacted high standards of conduct and courage from his followers. He was created from rock by Ormazd, Lord of Life, and was in eternal opposition to Ahriman, Lord of Death. Mithras was the ally of the Sun, with whom he became identified. It was he who slew a bull, and from the bull's blood and seed flowed corn and plenty; after the slaughter the first humans were born, and Mithras saved them from Ahriman. Worshippers of Mithras would growl like lions and crow like birds in their temples, wear animal masks, and had to undergo initiation ordeals.

Due to his Herculean personality, Mithras appealed particularly to soldiers, especially officers – hence the concentration of Mithraic temples near Hadrian's Wall. Women were excluded from the cult, which had no

Roman sculpture of the Birth of Mithras from Housesteads

Roman ivory clasp handle from South Shields

need of priests. This was a potent mystery religion, which gives added fascination to these remains from Mithraic temples. One of the altars depicts Mithras seizing the bull, and was set up by Lucius Sentius Castus, centurion of the Sixth Legion. Another altar shows Mithras holding the whip of the Sun god, round his head the Sun god's crown, the rays of which were illuminated by a lamp placed behind the altar in the temple; this altar was set up by Marcus Simplicius Simplex, prefect. 'The Birth of Mithras' relief was discovered in 1822, still in situ in the Mithraeum at Housesteads. It depicts Mithras being born from an egg, holding sword and torch, the twelve signs of the zodiac being carved in the egg-shaped frame. This is a stunning sculpture, which has been described as the most important Mithraic stone in Britain.

Other gods represented on the museum's inscriptions and reliefs include Neptune, Mars and Hercules, and an endearingly primitive Venus attended by water-nymphs. The gods Hercules and Antenociticus are portrayed in powerful carved stone heads.

The museum also has some carved heads of a native Celtic god with horns.

Several other items stand out among the Roman collections, some of them everyday things, others rare and delicate. The former include a hoard of bronze cooking vessels, which were once used by a Roman cavalry unit; a bronze wine-strainer from Whitfield Moor; leather from the Carrawburgh Mithraeum; and an iron-shod oak pile from the Roman bridge at Newcastle. Among the latter are two cameos, one made of sardonyx and depicting a bear (ill. on cover), the other agate showing Cupid astride a rearing horse; both are absolutely timeless. Two more pieces deserve special mention: the decorated bronze cheekpiece from a helmet showing one of the Heavenly Twins (Castor and Pollux), and a knife-handle of ivory carved in the form of a gladiator.

Of the later material three stone crosses have pride of place: the Rothbury Cross of about 800 AD, the Nunnykirk Cross of about 900 AD, and the Alnmouth Cross of the early 10th century.

Museum of Science and Engineering

Blandford House, Blandford Square,
Newcastle upon Tyne, Tyne and Wear
NE1 4JA   (091) 232 6789
Closed Sundays and Mondays.
F &W
& book in advance, contact
Education Department, ext. 449.

The Armstrong gun

The history of science is full of the most bizarre stories and characters, with many more failures than successes, the genius far outnumbered by the crackpot. True inventive genius has not been uncommon on Tyneside, as recognised in this museum.

Foremost among Tyneside engineers was William George Armstrong (1810–1900), inventor of the hydraulic crane and the hydraulic accumulator – not bad for a solicitor. It was Armstrong's factory at Elswick that built the machinery to operate Tower Bridge in London, and in 1876 built the Tyne Swing Bridge, then the largest swing bridge in the world. Examples of some of his early engines and machines are exhibited in the museum.

Armstrong's real fame, however, rests on his manufacture of guns and warships. It was he who developed the idea of enlarging the rifle to the size of a field gun, and of using an elongated projectile of lead instead of cast-iron balls. By 1858 the 18 lb Armstrong Gun, accurate over 1000 yards, was changing the nature of land warfare, and henceforth from Armstrong's works flowed a series of improved weaponry fit to arm Imperialist Britain.

During the 1860s Armstrong began manufacturing warships to take his big breechloading guns. HMS 'Victoria' was built in 1885, the world's most powerful warship, carrying 16¼in, 110 ton breechloading guns. Armstrong, and after his death his company, continued making a variety of armaments, including torpedoes, tanks, airships and aeroplanes. During the First World War the firm of Armstrong Whitworth employed no fewer than 78,000 people, 21,000 of them women. Armstrong's achievements are recorded here through models, photographs and full-size exhibits.

Another great Tyneside-based inventor was Charles Algernon Parsons (1854–1931). He developed the steam turbine, which revolutionised the generating of electricity and the means of powering ships. In 1894 Parsons built the world's first steam turbine-powered ship, the 100 ft 'Turbinia'. In 1897 this vessel achieved a world record speed of 34½ knots. By 1906 turbines were gigantic, powering vessels such as the battleship HMS 'Dreadnought' and, soon, the liner 'Mauretania'. Present-day turbines can exceed 800,000 kilowatts, over 1 million horsepower.

Women machine shop workers, 1917

Parsons's interests were wide, and in 1904 he developed the extraordinary Auxetophone, a machine to amplify the sound of musical instruments using compressed air. His invention was resisted by the Musicians' Union, whose members feared this attempt to reduce the number of players in a symphony orchestra. One cello concert was mounted in 1909 using the auxetophone.

The 'Eunice' horizontal steam engine of 1899

Parsons's 'Auxetophone'

A 90cm semi-parabolic mirror as used in searchlights is another example of Parsons's work. This gives the weirdest optical effects – see yourself as never before!

A gallery entitled 'Dugout to Dreadnought' dwells upon Tyneside's maritime past, largely one of shipbuilding. There is a host of models of coal-carrying vessels through the centuries, with displays illustrating life aboard ship. Other models include a Newcastle Galley of about 1295, a Viking Coaster of about 1000 AD, based on Skuldelev Ship 3, and a floating pontoon hospital of 1886. In the midst of the models is a full-size vessel, a small logboat of unknown date that was found in the river Tyne.

The 20th century models are larger in scale. Outstanding is HMS 'Nelson', sister ship of HMS 'Rodney', which was initially the flagship of the Home Fleet, and was in action throughout the Second World War. The model passenger liner RMS 'Mauretania' is here too, with some fittings and contents from the ship itself, notably a marble statue of 'Columbia' from the First Class Lounge. Larger than either of these is a scale model, fifteen yards long, of the river Tyne, showing docks, factories, shipbuilding yards and bridges. This was first exhibited in the Palace of Industries at the Great North East Coast Exhibition of 1929.

The Motive Power Gallery begins with the ancient Egyptians, rowing and sailing, and ends with Rolls Royce Conway jet engines. Along the way there are models of windmills, engines, pumps, traction engines, steam rollers and locomotives. Real items are also here in quantity, especially engines and pumps. 'Eunice' is a horizontal steam engine of 1899, which used to run a laundry in Rochdale. The Duplex Beam Blowing Engine of 1870, meanwhile, operated the organ stops of the Great Organ in the Albert Hall, London (sometimes I really do wonder how museum collections get to be where they are . . . this is in fact a loan from the National Museum of Science and Industry)

The Armstrong Whitworth motor car of 1911 (colour plate 3) is one of only five survivors of its ilk, and stands alongside the oldest surviving fire engine in the North East (on loan from Hull), purchased in 1753.

The Science Factory at the Museum of Science & Engineering is the North East's first permanent 'interactive' science centre, where the public can use exhibits to demonstrate principles of light, sound and energy. Strictly speaking, these science centres are not museums, because they do not have real things of historic value or interest. Nevertheless, they are an extension of what museums of science try to explain, and have a legitimate place in museums.

Newcastle's Science Factory allows you to generate watts on a pedalling machine, create soundwaves, conduct heat and study stress in plastic. The breeziest exhibit is that demonstrating the Bernoulli effect of air flow. For the narcissists among you, the hall of mirrors is sheer ecstacy!

PICKERING

Beck Isle Museum of Rural Life

Pickering, North Yorkshire YO18 8DU
(0751) 73653
Closed November to March, and
lunchtimes except during August. ▣
ᵫ **ST**: wheelchair access to
ground floor and yard only.
🛉 & 🛉 must book in advance.

By the banks of a clear trout stream
stands a stone-built Regency house
once inhabited by William Marshall
(1745–1818), who turned it into England's first Agricultural Institute. It is
now the home of a popular museum,
which gives a picture of changes in
rural life around the market town of
Pickering since Marshall's time.

Running through the museum displays like a thread of gold are the
photographs of that brilliant photographer, Sydney Smith of Pickering
(1884–1958). Far less fêted than Frank
Meadow Sutcliffe, the Whitby photographer born some thirty years before
him, Smith has left us with an almost
unparalleled documentary of the region he lived in and obviously loved all
of his life. Here, in photographs, is
captured the essence of the age of the
home and the village shop as truly as in
Fred Kitchen's *Brother to the Ox*, or
Flora Thompson's *Lark Rise to Candle-
ford*, and more honestly than in many of
Sutcliffe's romanticised confections.

Apart from Smith's photographs,
which alone are worth a visit to Beck
Isle, there are homely displays on a
number of themes, mostly of local
items, but with the occasional surprise.
Among the latter is a vase salvaged
from the Great Fire of Chicago (October 7th–10th 1871), and a Zulu necklace and fly whisk presented to the
museum by a retired missionary.
Slightly less exotic, but no less foreign
to this museum, is a Western Electric
35 mm projector head from the Empire
Cinema, Whitby, in use from 1934–84!
More expected is a Columbian

Exterior view of Beck Isle Museum of Rural Life

printing press of 1854 (which the
museum continues to use to produce
posters). But again there are reminders
in the printing room that even somewhere as 'Yorkshire' as Pickering was
prey to alien influences – the poster,
for example, of 1924 advertising a Café

Chantant at the local memorial hall
(admission 6d). Other images of the
continent are conjured up by the highly
collectable and unutterably sad little
cards produced by soldiers on the
Western Front in the First World War
to send to loved ones at home.

Butter-making equipment in the Dairy

The Police section features a broadsheet well worthy of today's tabloid press, entitled 'Horrible Murder and Mutilation of the Bodies of Joseph Wood and his Son', dated 1872:

'They searched the fields in all directions,
With pick and spade turned up the land,
At last beneath some muddy water,
They saw the murder'd farmer's hand;
They found the feet and parts of clothing,
A sad and sick'ning sight to see,
The remainder of the decaying body
Was buried beneath an old oak tree.'

Joseph's son is said to have been fed to pigs, not an unknown mode of disposing of bodies in rural areas.

The agricultural theme continues through the dairy (milk yokes, smocks, milkmaid's bonnet, churns) and the veterinary display, with its instruments that mostly seem to be for chopping bits off livestock, usually in the nether regions. The museum has a good collection of model farm vehicles and similar, including a 'Romany Living Wagon'. Hidden among these models is a full-size goat cart, fit to carry six children, and an extremely uncomfortable-looking tricycle made in 1869. Elsewhere there are ploughs, harrows, farm wagons, a chick incubator, shepherds' crooks, and a collection of other farming paraphernalia. Always the most gruesome among the relics of livestock husbandry are the pig-killing implements – the scalding trough, the killing-punch, the caumerills. Pigs are intelligent creatures, but humans have been devouring them for thousands of years.

The blacksmith, wheelwright, brushmaker, barber and cobbler are represented along with other crafts. At the Station Hotel the price of a pint of bitter has just gone up from 1s 4d to 1s 5d; local brewers like C. Rose of Malton, and the Scarborough & Whitby Breweries are still going strong. Among the chemist's wares is an advertisement for a contraption that rolls wheels over your body to smooth away 'the horrors of indigestion'. Eye-watering fare is a wholesale price list for, among other things, a truss for a scrotal hernia costing £1.8s.0d per dozen. Ouch!

A gent's outfitters and a costume

The bar at the Station Hotel

Interior view of the village shop

room feature clothing of different periods, best among which is Miss Piper's dress of about 1810. A children's room has lots of christening robes, with a toy farm, dolls, books, and some early 20th century German tinplate toys. A village shop crammed with groceries of all ages, a natural history display of birds' eggs and nests, butterflies, owls, and mammals, and a hardware shop all add to the variety of this museum.

My favourite item at Beck Isle is the giant quilt made by teachers, pupils and friends of St Peter's Church Sunday School, Pickering, in 1888, when little girls had names like Cissy Nawton, Ada Hesp, Agnes Flood and Gertie Robertson. These and scores of other names have been loving stitched onto the quilt, where they conjure up more visions of the Victorian Pickering so well illustrated in other parts of the museum.

SCUNTHORPE

Scunthorpe Museum and Art Gallery

Oswald Road, Scunthorpe, South Humberside DN15 7BD
(0724) 843533
Open daily. ▣
♿ ST: wheelchair access to ground floor only, steps between levels and into building negotiable by museum's portable ramps.
⚐ & ⚐ book in advance: contact Receptionist. If talks or similar required book at least 2 weeks in advance: contact Education Officer. ◉

Into deepest South Humberside or, if you are a traditionalist, deepest North Lincolnshire, an area rich in history, as a visit to Scunthorpe Museum will show, for those who can be tempted from the regular tourist trails.

Scunthorpe is a town made up of five separate vilages, each with its own history, and did not exist as a town much before 1900. Its growth was based on local availability of iron-ore bearing rock, and much of the town's history is based on the development of the iron and steel industries, although the area around has a much older story to tell. The museum is fittingly housed in an old Vicarage that was built in 1875 from local ironstone.

Scunthorpe's local history galleries are very typical of modern museum display, in that there is much to read and lots of photographs, as well as the object collections themselves. Sections are included on Pubs, Education, Toys, Tobacco and Smoking, Home Entertainment, Sport, Feasts and Fairs, Folklore, and other subjects. In cramming such a range into a relatively small space, the museum is able to give us tantalising glimpses of past life.

We have the familiar gas masks, bottles, truncheons, samplers and toys (including a nice dolls' house with push-button lighting), but we can also see jet and vulcanite jewellery, cock-

Burringham Plough 'Jag' hobby horse with hood

spurs, a Victorian mandoline harp, and a 1925 Revophone Crystal Set. The Laundry section reminds us that in North Lincolnshire pig urine was regarded as a most effective whitening agent! Ugh!

The Folklore section is especially lively, featuring as it does a Fool's Costume from the Willoughton Plough Play, and a hobby-horse complete with hood from the Burringham Plough 'Jag'. This is a region where old customs tend to die hard, and the tale is told here of the Haxey Hood, wherein

teams contest for possession of a rolled tube of leather, a tradition said to date from the 13th century when Lady Mowbray lost her hood at Haxey. The event has its own Lord, its Fool and its 'Chief Boggan', and the museum has a Lord's Wand made of thirteen willows bound round thirteen times.

One of my favourite bits of any museum is the Recent Accession case – you never know what treasure or horror you will see! On one visit to Scunthorpe there was an early Victorian Electric Shock Machine for Nervous Disorders, and a lovely Back and Kidney Pills Box of Stotherts Ltd. Other Stothert products available, according to the lid, included pills for Blood and Stomach, Liver and Kidney, 'Females' (for female ailments), and compound Rhubarb pills.

The archaeology galleries have an impressive collection on view, as befits a region so steeped in history. Among the earliest items is the Bronze-Age Appleby Logboat, dated to 1100 BC, and found in 1943 on the bed of the River Ancholme, where it had been known for some years as an obstruction in the river! The boat was preserved there for 3,000 years because of the waterlogged, airless conditions.

The gallery resonates with evocative placenames, mostly Viking in origin. The Bagmoor Hoard of late Bronze Age metalwork, found in 1933 in an ironstone mine, is in remarkable condition, and is part of a larger display of prehistoric bronzes. The display of objects found during excavations at Dragonby includes fine Iron Age pottery of the Corieltauvi tribe, and the Romano-British metalwork features brooches, finger-rings, bracelets, pins and a lone earring, as well as strangely-decorated bucket mounts from the Thealby hoard.

The extent and importance of the Roman Empire is brought home, as in so many other museums, by various fascinating fragments: a piece of a

Tudor carved stone head of a lady from Scotter

limestone column, painted wallplaster and a mosaic, for example, from a Roman villa at Winterton, discovered in 1797. Oddest of all, to our modern eyes, is the collection of Roman phallic amulets, including a bold, ivory winged phallus from Crosby. The phallus was a good luck charm symbolising virility, strength and fertility, and the wings brought added speed!

Anglo-Saxon items, like a bronze bowl from Manton inlaid with glass and enamel, reflect the richness of the Kingdom of Lindsey, within which South Humberside lay. From the medieval and post medieval periods, Scunthorpe has spurs, keys, scissors, buckles, spade shoes, and a host of other everyday items found in rubbish pits, in fields, or on building sites. There is a delightful carved stone head of a lady, probably from a family monument once in Scotter church and dating from the late Tudor period. Also from a church, this time St Mary's at Barnetby-le-Wold, is a splendid lead

font. Holes were drilled through it in the 13th century, when it was already 100 years old, to secure the lid (which is now missing) to prevent the theft of holy water for use in black magic . . .

Natural history is the third main gallery at Scunthorpe, and here you can see specimens of wildlife from North Lincolnshire, combined with fossils, minerals and rocks. Memorable for me was an otter, and ammonites turned green by a coating of the iron mineral chamosite. The gallery has a welcome 'touch and stroke' geology section, which includes 150-million-year-old tree trunks, giant ammonites and ancient sand ripples. As befits a town so dependent on iron ore, the museum has good geology collections.

In addition, temporary exhibitions of art, craft and photography are regularly shown, and the museum has a small art collection, including local works that prove that even the steel-encrusted Scunthorpe skyline can stir the artist in the human soul.

Stotherts Ltd pill tin

SHEFFIELD

Bishops' House

Meersbrook Park, Norton Lees Lane, Sheffield, South Yorkshire S8 9BE
(0742) 557701
Closed Mondays and Tuesdays. ⬛
& **S**: wheelchair access to ground floor only.
🚻 & 🚻 should book in advance: contact Keeper/Assistant Keeper, Social and Labour History. Prebooked 🚻 from Sheffield LEA ⬛. ☺

The building itself is the most splendid exhibit. Erected around 1500 it is the most complete timber-framed house in Sheffield, with many 16th and 17th century features. The legend is that two Blythe brothers, John, Bishop of Salisbury (1494–99) and Geoffrey, Bishop of Lichfield and Coventry (1503–33) lived here as youths, although there is no evidence of this. It is a farmhouse, no more, and is a reminder of far-off days when Sheffield was a market town surrounded by fields, and when the river Sheaf ran clear.

It is known, however, that one William Blythe lived here, and his initials are carved with the date 1627 in some panelling in the Hall. Blythe, a farmer, died in 1631, leaving silver, pewter and brassware, with carpets, curtains and bedhangings among his most valuable possessions. He also owned no fewer than 1,900 scythes, and may have been the largest local producer of scythes prior to the Civil War. Blythe is an example of the type of man whose efforts later spawned the giant iron and steel industry of the area.

There are several interesting features of the building, including decorative plasterwork over two of the fireplaces, probably the work of local craftsmen, which includes favourite fruits of the early 17th century, such as grapes and figs. The panelling in the Hall is richly carved with strapwork motifs, and shows Flemish influence.

Two of the rooms are furnished as they might have been in the 17th century. On the ground floor the Great Parlour contains fine oak furniture, including a table and chairs, and the bed-chamber on the first floor has a joined oak tester bedstead of 1620–50, and an oak cradle of 1620.

The rest of the historic collections are a pot pourri of 17th century life in and around Tudor and Stuart Sheffield. The section on the poor is, naturally enough, small, because so little material has survived: the knucklebone apple-corer, boar's tusk lamp and horn tinder box are odd fragmentary remnants of a distant way of life. Odder still are bone ice-skates, used in the winter of 1685 when the rivers and millponds of Sheffield froze over.

An elaborate carved oak overmantel from Greenhill Hall introduces us to

Oak overmantel from Greenhill Hall, 17th century

Christopher Wilson's gloves

Wilson family christening basket, 17th century

gentrified life in the 17th century, a few steps up the social scale from the Blythes who lived in Bishops' House. There are Christopher Wilson's handsome gloves ; Ann Wilson's wedding gloves; a Wilson christening basket; and a Wilson gentleman's cap, replete with blackwork embroidery, sequins and gold lace, worn when sitting in bed. A strongbox, a silver porringer, a 1606 drinking horn, a pair of archer's gloves, and a set of ebony domino playing cards all hint at various 17th century preoccupations of the gentry.

In very good condition is a small collection of military items, including a Cavalier's boot from Haddon Hall, 17th century saddlebags, a Cavalier's saddle from Scarborough Castle, and a 16th century crossbow and bolts.

Most intriguing of all are the objects associated with local customs and beliefs. There are the uniform and swords of the Handsworth Sword Dance, a local long-sword dancing tradition dating to 1887, performed at Christmas by eight men who link swords, eventually forming a knot of swords. At one time all the dancers were coal miners, and the Handsworth team was known as the 'dancing miners'.

The sole of a shoe and a horse blinker found buried in the wall of a 17th century Bradshaw farm were supposed, respectively, to bring good luck to the building and to avert the

Drinking horn, 1606

Evil Eye. A Witch Stone, a lucky stone with holes in it, kept witches away. A devil's head made in plasterwork from Copley Hall, of about 1630, a 17th century clog almanac from Barnsley, marked out with each day of the year, and a doll in a milly box, which used to be taken from door to door on Boxing Day by girls who sang 'Here we come a

wassailing among the leaves so green', give more insights into ways of life very different from those of today.

Lastly, there is a remnant of another way of life thankfully long gone: the brank or scold's bridle, used to restrain the tongues of 'gossiping women' – rare is the museum that does not have one.

Mappin Art Gallery

Weston Park, Sheffield, South Yorkshire S10 2TP   (0742) 726281
Closed Mondays. 🇫 ▣   ⚐ W
🛗 & 🚻 book in advance. ◎

Some of the foremost artists of the past 200 years are represented in the collections of Sheffield City Art Galleries, a changing selection of which are displayed at the Mappin, and at the *Graves Art Gallery* (items described below may be on display at either venue – check in advance if you want to see a specific work). The collections are particularly strong in British paintings, but also feature some fine continental works.

Among the latter, French artists stand out. Paul Cézanne is probably the pre-eminent painter of the past century. His 'Bassin du Jas de Bouffan' is a dark landscape painted at his house in Provence. The great Impressionist painter Pierre Auguste Renoir is represented here by 'La Rivière' (1878; on loan), which illustrates a phase of his life when his paintings laid down light in colour with no firm outlines. Marie Cazin was also influenced by the Impressionists, as her 'Outskirts of Abbeville' shows. Pierre Bonnard painted many nudes, and his 'Nude with Black Stockings' (on loan) is one of the most sensuous. Earlier than any of these are some works by the 19th century landscape painter, Jean Corot, including 'Au Petit Chaville'.

The Dutchman Aert van der Neer was a 17th century artist noted for his nocturnal landscapes and his winter scenes. The Mappin's 'Frozen River Scene' is typical of the latter. 'Winter Landscape' by Thomas Heeremans is a slightly later painting in the same tradition. Quite different from these Old Masters is Waagen's 'The Keppel Shepherds', a 19th century sculpture – the only one in the original collections put together by J.N. and F.T. Mappin – depicting a hunter on horseback holding up a lion's head, his dogs in attendance, a sheep slung across the horse's back. Another foreign artist, Wassily Kandinsky, was born in Moscow, but became one of the first abstract painters based in Munich. His

Paul Cézanne, Bassin du Jas de Bouffan, *c.1873–76*

J. M. W. Turner, Macon – The Festival of the Opening of the Vintage, *first exhibited 1803*

'Two Riders Against Red' is a small but bold colour composition of red, green, blue and yellow.

J.M.W. Turner is without doubt the greatest British painter. The Mappin Art Gallery has a number of his works

(and anyone particularly interested in the period should visit the Mappin's sister gallery, the *Ruskin Gallery*). 'Maçon – The Festival of the Opening of the Vintage' has dancing in the foreground, with a river and bridge,

Sir Edward Burne-Jones, The Hours, *1882*

and a landscape beyond. It was painted before Turner began fully to explore how to show effects of light and atmosphere in paint; nevertheless, the sun glows here behind the clouds. 'Brinkburn Priory on the River Coquet' has a stranger play of light, with creamy trees and ground surface, and dark-grey flowing water. More impressionistic are 'Storm off the East Coast' and 'Seascape with Boat'.

W. Clarkson Stanfield's 'The Morning After the Wreck' is altogether a more realistic painting, the value of which has fluctuated with the popularity of such Victorian art. This is an epic work showing the aftermath of a shipwreck, the stricken sailing ship still afloat but broken-masted, a variety of small boats with survivors and rescuers bobbing all around her in a turbulent sea. Walter Horsley's 'The French in Cairo' is another impressive Victorian work, showing Napoleon's soldiers in Cairo carving French titles on monuments. Two more notable paintings of the 19th century are 'The Proposal' by J.E. Millais, in which a monumentally bored-looking woman receives the attentions of a spidery suitor, who is kicking away a dog (an artistic symbol of fidelity), and 'The Hours' by Edward Burne-Jones, a striking example of that artist's particular style.

Walt Disney, Snow White and the Prince

20th century British works cover a wide range of media and styles. William Rothenstein's 'Buffer Girls' is a dignified portrait study of women who worked in the Sheffield steel industry. William Nicholson was noted for his portraits and still-lifes, but his 'Road to Zamaramala' is a chalky-coloured landscape. 'A Corner of the Artist's Room, Paris, c. 1907–10' by Gwen John is a haunting interior of the artist's room at 87 rue du Cherche-Midi, with a table, wicker chair, parasol, flowers, and view through a window (colour plate 5). Gwen's flam-

boyant brother, Augustus John, was a brilliant portraitist, as exemplified by his 'Señora Gañdarillas'.

Paul Nash is perhaps most renowned for his records of First and Second World War scenes. His landscapes have a striking originality: 'Iver Heath, Snow' is dominated by stark trees; 'Grotto in the Snow' (on loan) is almost monochromatic. Stanley Spencer was another original painter, whose 'Helter Skelter' has its monumental multi-coloured wooden tower climbing into the sky. Harry Epworth Allen gives an unusual and distinctive treatment to 'Derbyshire Walls'. Henry Moore, the most famous of modern British sculptors, is represented in the Mappin by 'Mother and Child' (on loan from the Henry Moore Foundation).

Among more contemporary pieces, 'Minuet' by Tess Jaray is made up of geometric shapes in pastel blue and pink, while 'Rise 1' by Bridget Riley consists of horizontal stripes of white, orange, green and lilac, and will make your eyes go funny!

If all this fine British art is too much for you, there is a real curiosity: 'Snow White and the Prince' (with doves, of course) by the great American animator, Walt Disney. Not very challenging but *ever* so sweet.

Sheffield City Museum

Weston Park, Sheffield, South Yorkshire S10 2TP (0742) 768588
Open daily. **F** **&** **W**
† & **†** should book in advance:
contact Extension Services staff. ◎

Lots to see here, in this museum in the North East's largest city, famed for its iron and steel industry. In this building are housed collections of cutlery, decorative arts, archaeology, ethnography and natural history – a typical 'city museum', if you like, whose approach to display would not shock a Victorian visitor.

Most unusual among these collections is the cutlery, to which there is devoted a whole gallery. Here you can see the oldest Sheffield knife known to exist, dating from the 14th century and found at Sheffield Castle. Every conceivable type of knife, fork and spoon is on show, with a few less conceivable items in the 'Curious Cutlery' section, like an asparagus eater and a pea-eating knife. This is a penknife paradise, with a blade or other tool for all occasions; if you thought the Swiss Army had all the ideas, think again!

The Applied Arts Gallery is full of metalware and pottery, with the emphasis on locally-made pieces. Take your choice from fused plate, electroplate, Britannia metal, even brass – tea urns, tea and coffee sets, tea caddies, teapots, wine coolers, cruets, ink stands, egg stands, sauce boats, christening mugs, a baby's feeding bottle, candlesticks, snuffer trays, toast racks, cheese toasters, bottle stands, snuff boxes, tankards, mugs, dinner plates, dishes, sugar basins, tobacco jars, powder flasks, claret jugs, mustard pots, milk jugs, a Russian samovar . . . the list is exhausting, and if nothing else proves that we British take our table-setting seriously, even if our food has not always matched up to what we serve it on! Of especial note among the metalwares are a tortoise-shaped soup tureen, and a coffee machine of 1850 by Padley, Parkin and Staniforth of Sheffield.

Old Sheffield Plate turtle soup tureen, c.1800

Ivory knife handles, from a set of 12 knives, German, c.1600

The pottery collection is far less comprehensive, but is worth seeing, and runs through a wide range from early salt-glazed stoneware, English delftware and slipware, to more modern items. Leeds pottery, Rockingham porcelain and Staffordshire pottery are among the most interesting pieces, pride of place going to a 1740 bear jug, covered in shreds of clay to imitate fur, with detachable head to serve as a drinking cup. Far less useful are the china souvenirs of the First World War – tanks, field guns, aeroplanes, despatch riders, ambulances, even warships, including submarines. Finally, there is the collection of plates, jugs and mugs commemorating the Sheffield Flood of 1865, when the Dale Dyke Dam burst, claiming 258 lives.

Much of the strong archaeology collection was purchased in 1893 when the discoveries of local archaeologist

Thomas Bateman became available. Bateman was a voracious collector, one of whose best finds was the Benty Grange Anglo-Saxon Helmet of the 7th century AD, once owned by a warrior of the Pecsaetan (Peak Dwellers). The helmet is crested with an ornamental boar of bronze body, gilded silver studs and hip plates, and gold and garnet eyes. The hip plates were cut from antique Roman silver plate. The boar is associated with the pagan god Frey, but the helmet also has a cross symbol on the nasal protector – a meeting, perhaps, of pagan and Christian beliefs. The helmet is displayed along with a modern replica, which shows the full glory of this outstanding piece (colour plates 7 & 8).

Other dramatic items include a 1st century AD bronze torc (neck-ring), which combines the local Brigantian and southern styles of decoration; and several carved stone heads, evidence of the Celtic belief in the magical power of the severed human head, which led them to hunt heads for display in their houses and temples. Viking, Norman and medieval collections complete the picture of the region before the steel industry came to predominate.

From further afield come the ethnography collections. In the displays it is possible to compare, for example, Eskimo spears and a Commanche Indian bow from Arizona with British Stone-Age tools. Extensive collections of knives and swords, meanwhile, demonstrate that Sheffield has not had a monopoly in this department.

Natural history is presented in two galleries, one entitled 'Evolution', the other 'World Wildlife'. Evolution is illustrated using collections of minerals, rocks and fossils, with human and gorilla skeletons displayed side by side. The past environment of the Sheffield area is also explained, centred around some mounted wildlife no longer, one is assured, to be found in the region, such as the Brown Bear and the Wolf.

Current wildlife is displayed according to its environment, so there are sections on moorland, woodland, grassland, freshwater and so on. Moths and butterflies, barn owls and badgers mingle with live fish and a colony of wood ants. Life in urban areas is not ignored, and the park, the churchyard and the refuse tip are shown to be ideal habitats for a host of creatures. We are reminded that man is the world's most

vicious predator, and the sad displays of the skull and tusks of the Asian Elephant, a Narwhal tusk and Sperm Whale teeth stand as silent reproof.

At the furry end of the evolutionary scale are a giant Polar Bear, a Chimpanzee, a Duck-Billed Platypus, a Marmoset, and a White-Faced Woodland Ram; at the creepy-crawly end are the Scorpion, the Giant Centipede and the Horseshoe Crab; somewhere in the middle (the really worrying bit) are the jaws of the White Shark and the skull of the Crocodile. Plants are here, too, including the double coconut, the world's largest seed.

16th century Iranian helmet

Completing the Museum displays is a corridor of miscellaneous treasures, such as a case of shoes, coins and tokens, Japanese swords, Indo-Iranian arms (including a wonderful 16th century Iranian helmet), and a collection of watches and clocks. Among the last is a remarkable Cortelazzo clock with steel and silver case, shown at the 1871 International Exhibition.

Take plenty of time to see the City Museum and the adjacent **Mappin Art Gallery**, which between them have collections of the greatest variety.

Old Sheffield Plate table, c.1825

STOCKTON-ON-TEES

Preston Hall Museum

Yarm Road, Stockton-on-Tees, Cleveland (0642) 781184
Open daily. **F** **P**
&. **ST**: wheelchair access to ground floor and Victorian street only.
⚭ & **⚭** book in advance: contact the Curator, Stockton-on-Tees Museums, PO Box 116, Gloucester House, 72 Church Road, Stockton-on-Tees, Cleveland TS18 1YB
(0642) 670067 (school bookings 0642 602474).

It is the dream of every museum curator to discover a lost masterpiece among his/her collections. It doesn't happen very often, but it did at Preston Hall in 1972. Twice.

It was during a routine inspection and valuation of the bequest of paintings to the people of Stockton made by Miss Annie Elizabeth Clephan in 1930. The paintings had belonged to her father, Edwin Clephan, a banker who was an avid collector of art. It was known that there were some distinguished works among the Clephan Bequest, such as Thomas Girtin's watercolour, 'River View', but there were two works whose significance had been completely overlooked. One of these was the small watercolour 'Mustering of the Warrior Angels' by J.M.W. Turner. This is a strange painting, which shows clearly the fascination with light of this, the greatest of British painters.

Even more astounding was the second discovery. Georges de la Tour (1593–1652) lived and worked all his life in Lorraine, France. As a painter, he was, like Turner, particularly interested in light and its effects, and was influenced in his style by the master of *chiaroscuro* (the balance of light and shadow), the Italian Caravaggio. In his later works, La Tour adopted forms of indirect lighting from concealed

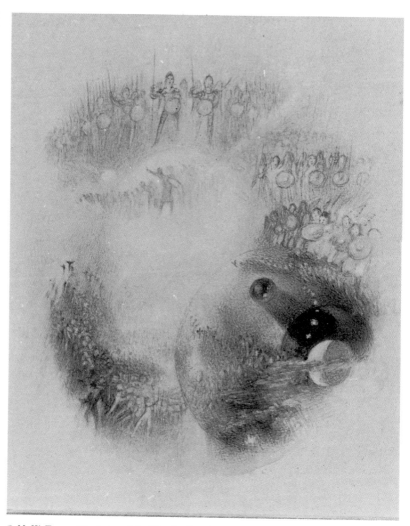

J. M. W. Turner, Mustering of the Warrior Angels, *watercolour*

sources. Just such a painting is 'The Dice Players' (colour plate 14) at Preston Hall, one of only three paintings by La Tour in Britain. The painting shows two young soldiers throwing dice, with three other figures looking on. Light from a candle, which is half-hidden by one of the dice player's arms, illuminates the scene, casting deep shadows, and reflecting brightly off the armour of the soldiers.

Another important bequest to Stockton was the G.O. Spence Bequest of 1925, notable for its snuff boxes, pewter, arms and armour, and

military medals. The range of the arms and armour is most impressive. Earlier weaponry includes collections of axes, with an enormous 17th or 18th century headman's axe, and maces, stunning weapons favoured by cavalry, of the 15th and 16th centuries. Military flails, hammers and pole axes are other fearsome weapons that pre-date the general introduction of firearms.

An extensive collection of swords, knives, daggers and bayonets complements the armour, which features a series of helmets, such as a German war hat of about 1575, a Cromwellian lobster-tailed helmet of about 1650, a burgonet of about 1600, and two morions, one German with embossed fleur-de-lys. Crossbows, pistols and other firearms, and a fine collection of powder flasks, all illustrate the meeting of violent intent with decorative art.

The snuff box is a most genuine relic of a lost age of elegance. The important thing about a snuff box was its appearance, and imagination was allowed to run riot with their design in the 18th century. G.O. Spence had hundreds of examples, and they make a bizarre display. Snuff boxes come in all materials – horn, ivory, tin, papier mâché, silver, brass, wood, tortoiseshell, shell, enamelled copper, gold. And they come in all sorts of shapes – pistols, shoes, hands, horses' heads, rams, coffins, and figures such as fiddle players. There are also some ordinary box shapes here, some of the nicest with painted scenes, such as Frederick the Great after his defeat at the Battle of Koline in 1757, and the appearance of the Fairy in the Palace of the White Cats. A wooden box is said to have been made from Shakespeare's mulberry tree, and another from the timber of old London Bridge.

Personal snuff rasps or graters gave another excuse for elaborate design, usually carved or inscribed wood or ivory, and many of them are of very high quality.

Pewter is an alloy of tin and lead or copper (or both), first made by the Romans, and commonly in use in Britain in the 17th and 18th centuries, after which it was largely replaced by pottery. Preston Hall has some fine pewter pieces, locally made and European. Edmund Harvey (1698–1781) was one local pewterer, and some of his wares are displayed, including flagons in the St Denis or Acorn style, with their domed lids and characteristically bulbous bodies. Other pieces include patens (plates), quaghs (small bowls with two lug ears), salts, candlesticks, spice canisters, measures, and later Victorian pewter items, such as a tea caddy, a spoon warmer and tavern mugs.

Many of the large and varied Preston Hall collections are displayed in period

Edmund Harvey pewter flagons, c.1780

rooms and a reconstructed Victorian Street of shops. Among the most successful of the rooms are the Victorian kitchen, the dressmaker's and the schoolroom. The street is actually built outside, and as such it is much more realistic than most similar displays. There are about twenty different premises, of which the more unusual are a taxidermist and a fruiterer, including the most convincing (and working) reconstructed blacksmith's and farrier's you are likely to see. Other highlights are the hatter (wonderful hats!), draper ('Funerals Conducted in a Most Careful Manner'), tobacconist, musical instrument dealer, grocer, chemist and fancy goods shop.

The costume section has welcome displays of men's clothing, as well as children's. Jewellery, embroidery, paisley shawls, beadwork, Berlin wool work, and items connected with hair grooming and writing form other strong collections.

In the attic is a host of children's toys and games, with train sets, card games, dolls, a toy farm, Escalado, Meccano, teddy bears, toy cars, rocking horses, books, and a Mr. Punch's Theatre. There is a Jiggle Joggle Frog race game, and a rare French monkey artist automaton. This last has an artist (a monkey) dressed in a satin pantaloon suit, sitting beneath a tree in blossom, his easel and portrait before him. His model is a simpering female monkey looking all the fashion. The caption explains that the artist dips his brush onto his palette, dabs at the portrait, and turns his head, 'baring his teeth at intervals', all to music. Those French!

Snuff mull, snuff box and snuff rasps, 17th–19th century

SUNDERLAND

Sunderland Museum and Art Gallery

Borough Road, Sunderland, Tyne and Wear SR1 1PP   (091) 514 1235
Closed Mondays, except Bank Holidays. 🅵 🖿 ♿
♿ & 🚻 contact Education Officer.
⊛

Sunderland Museum and Art Gallery has a little bit for everyone, with particularly strong collections of locally-made glass and pottery. The collections began to be assembled in the early 19th century, and Sunderland had the country's first municipal museum outside London.

Sunderland's potteries are most famous for their lustreware – pottery that has a metallic finish. Pottery was made on Wearside between the early 18th century and the 1950s, the industry having been based upon local coal to fire the kilns, local brown clay, and cheap river transport. It was only after the 1850s that competition from Staffordshire and abroad brought about a decline in Sunderland. The local industry was characterised by small family firms, and at its peak in 1850 it employed no more than 400 skilled workers, of whom sixty were women and forty-five children aged under fourteen.

The museum has a very comprehensive display of pottery from all the firms whose wares survive. The best among these are the pots made at Low Ford or Dawson's Pottery, from about 1794 to 1864, which include creamware as well as purple, copper and silver lustreware. The pink lustreware of the Sunderland or 'Garrison' pottery is also very fine. A typical piece of lustreware is a pink lustre jug of about 1815 with a view of the Iron Bridge at Sunderland (ill. on cover); when it opened this was the world's largest single-span iron bridge at 236 feet long and 100 feet above low water mark. Also worth looking out for in the display of English pottery and porcelain are Bow porcelain figures of 1765–66 of a boy and girl with flowers, and a number of finely-painted Worcester figures.

Like pottery manufacture, glassmaking began in Sunderland because of local coal and river transport, and also because local magnesian limestone was used in the process. Glassmaking sand was brought from King's Lynn by collier vessels returning from London and the continent. The manufacture began in the late 17th century, and the museum has early wineglasses and bottles of this period and slightly later. Window glass, cut glass, engraved glass and pressed glass were all made in Sunderland. Although the industry declined at the end of the 19th century, it is still a significant industry in the town.

Particularly associated with Sunderland is the special type of glassware known as 'Pyrex'. This is a brand name for borosilicate glass, which is very heat-resistant, and which was made in the town by James A. Jobling Ltd., under license from the American manufacturer, Corning, which took over the Sunderland factory in 1973. Pyrex has been produced in a host of forms, from ovenware and tableware to household decorations, and continues to be a popular product.

Pyrex coffee jug, c.1967

Madonna and Child, c.1500–30

Wearside's best-known industry, which ceased in 1989, was shipbuilding. The museum has a good collection of scale models of ships built in Sunderland, from full-rigged sailing ships to steam vessels, both cargo vessels and warships.

'The Sunderland Story' gallery shows a wide range of items that illustrate the town's history, and that of the region before the town existed. Among the archaeological exhibits are Bronze Age burials from the important Hasting Hill barrow, complete with skeletons, and Anglo-Saxon glass and other finds from excavations at St Peter's monastery, Monkwearmouth, companion to St Paul's monastery at **Jarrow**.

Other notable items from the pre-industrial period include a lovely wooden Madonna and Child of 1500–30, some Civil War armour and a pair of 17th century boots, and the Lumley hoard of silver coins, probably buried for safekeeping at the time of the invasion of England by the Scots in 1644.

Pride of place from the 19th century goes to two well-known local characters, one a sailor, the other a lion.

The sailor was Jack Crawford, born in Sunderland. During the naval Battle of Camperdown between the British and Dutch fleets in 1797, he nailed the colours of Admiral Duncan to the broken mast of the flagship, HMS 'Venerable', so that the rest of the fleet would not think that Duncan had surrendered and lowered his colours. Crawford became a national hero, and the monument to him in the museum is a life-size figure of Crawford performing his heroic deed. It is carved like a ship's figurehead, and once graced a pub.

Wallace was the 450 lb lion who, on a visit to Sunderland in 1868 with William Mander's Grand National Star Menagerie, attacked his 'tamer', one Martini Maccomo. Perhaps Wal-

Wallace the Lion, once the star of William Mander's menagerie

Jack Crawford (miniature of the Mowbray Park statue by Percy Wood)

lace mistook Martini for food, as he (Martini) was dressed in war-paint with a head-dress of blue and scarlet macaw feathers. Martini and Wallace both survived the ordeal, and Wallace lived until 1875 when he died in Warrington, ending up on show in Sunderland in 1879, where he has been ever since.

Of more than passing interest is a walrus, once said to have been the inspiration for Lewis Carroll's *The Walrus and the Carpenter* ('fit to snore his head off! as Tweedledum remarked'). In fact, the Walrus's head was parted from its body in 1965 because the latter had deteriorated. The head survives, possibly still reflecting on the Sunderland Museum and Library Committee's decision in 1875 that 'the Curator have authority to get the Walrus stuffed by some person' . . .

Another exhibit marks the tragic death of 191 children in Victoria Hall, Sunderland, in 1883. Over 2000 children had packed the hall to see Mr Fay the magician, who began to give away free gifts. In the rush to get themselves toys, children raced down stairs that led to a door which was bolted ajar, and in a hauntingly familiar way, those at the front were crushed by the pressure of those behind. One of the toys, a

small wooden horse with its front legs broken off, was subsequently sent to the museum by a relative of a little girl who escaped the tragedy.

A Geology gallery looks at the Sunderland region, focussing on Frosterley Marble, a local stone used for columns in the Chapel of Nine Altars in Durham Cathedral; the cannonball

Fossil of Coelurosauravus

Clarkson Stanfield, The Castle of Ischia, *1841*

WAKEFIELD

Wakefield Art Gallery

Wentworth Terrace, Wakefield, West Yorkshire WF1 3QW
(0924) 375402
Open daily. **F**
& S: wheelchair access to ground floor only; steps at entrance – staff will assist to lift wheelchairs.
& ♂ contact Education Officer.
☺

Britain's two greatest sculptors were born within five years and a few miles of each other in Yorkshire, one in Castleford, the other in Wakefield. Both were trained at Leeds College of Art. They are Henry Moore and Barbara Hepworth, and both are represented by a number of important works in Wakefield Art Gallery.

Moore (1898–1986) centred his work on humanity and the human figure, and although he is best known for his sculptures, he also drew a great deal. His 'Shelter' drawings were commissioned by the War Artists' Advisory Committee during the London Blitz. A powerful, emotive drawing at Wakefield from this series is 'Figure in a Shelter', showing a prone woman under a blanket raising herself on her arms in the gloom of the London Underground. Her head is unnaturally small, her arms unnaturally spindly, the whole is hallucinatory.

Of the same wartime period are Moore's 'Mining' series of drawings – studies of miners, mostly at the coalface. Wakefield has 'Coal Miner Using Heading Machine in Drift' and 'Miners at the Coalface', both of which show bodies kneeling and twisted as they strive to work the coal. A third drawing from the series, 'Pit Boys at Pit Head', is a study of four helmeted heads in the same media of pencil, ink, charcoal, wax crayon and wash as the others. Moore himself regarded this particular drawing as the finest in his series of mining drawings.

Three completely different styles of Moore's three-dimensional work are

limestone, a fossilised barrier reef; the only British example of an Upper Permian-period gliding reptile, known as *Coelurosauravus jaekeli*, which was found in 1878. This is the oldest known (and most unpronounceable) vertebrate animal capable of gliding flight.

A Local Wildlife gallery features lots of varieties of birds, mammals and fish, some of the latter alive in tanks. Bats, rats, foxes, badgers, weasels, puffins, owls, kestrels, crabs, lobsters, frogs, toads – they are all here. The ugliest exhibit is the Angler Fish. As its caption politely puts it, 'its broad head has a wide gaping mouth with large curved teeth'. There are also displays on conservation and the protection of the environment.

The art collection is, like the rest of the museum, varied. Paintings worth studying include 'Easter Day at Rome' by John Frederick Lewis (1805–76) and 'The Castle of Ischia' by Sunderland-born Clarkson Stanfield (1828–78), with its dramatic foreground shipwreck under glowering skies, the castle high up in the background illuminated by the sun through a break in the clouds. Two local paintings by John Wilson Carmichael (1800–68) are 'Old Hartlepool' and 'Murton Colliery', while three works

Optic for the Roker lighthouse

by L.S. Lowry (1887–1976) were also inspired by local townscapes. A touch of romance is brought by 'The Little Truant' by Hector Caffieri (1847–*c.* 1911).

Finally, there are the fog siren and lamp from Roker Pier Lighthouse. The 'lamp' is a six-foot wide glass optic, which makes a fitting entrance to the museum galleries. Think of the lives it has saved.

Henry Moore, Reclining Figure, *1936*

represented by three sculptures. The earliest is the concrete 'Head of a Woman' (1926), executed not long after he left the Royal College of Art when he was particularly influenced by African and Pre-Columbian Mexican art. 'Reclining Figure' in elmwood, of 1936, has a hole punctured through the chest – Moore's first use of a hole in an unexpected place to emphasise the three-dimensional nature of his sculptures. 'Reclining Figure No.4', of 1961, is cast in bronze, but continues his fascination with the human form.

Hepworth (1903–75), like Moore, did not restrict herself entirely to sculpture. Her 'Tibia Graft' is a pencil and oil work in which the eyes of the surgeon dominate, concentrating above his mask on the task in hand. 'Genesis III' is an abstract oil and pencil work on wood of 1966. 'Kneeling Figure' in rosewood of 1932 is a female figure on

Barbara Hepworth, Tibia Graft, *1949*

Barbara Hepworth, Mother and Child, *1934*

one knee, hands clasped. 'Pierced Hemisphere 1', a silky-smooth study in white marble of 1937, shows Hepworth's own use of a hole to open up a closed form. Her 'Mother and Child' is a masterpiece of 1934 in pink ancaster stone, the child standing in its mother's lap in timeless harmony.

James Tissot, The Thames, *1876*

While Wakefield's main strength lies in 20th century works, there are some good earlier paintings, oils and watercolours. For me, the best of the oils was 'Still Life with Lobster' by Nicolaes van Verendael (1640–91), brilliantly coloured with fruits, butterflies, flowers, rosé wine and a snail (colour plate 12). 'Poultry in a Farmyard', attributed to Aelbert Cuyp, a great 17th century Dutch landscape painter, shows a proud cockerel with four hens, a disappearing cat on a barrel, and a lurking hedgehog. More sombre than either of these is another 17th century Dutch painting, 'Still Life with Lemon' by Jacob van Es, this one with white wine. 'The Sacrifice' by Jan van Huysum (1682–1749) is a classical scene by an artist better known for his flower pictures. A 'Classical Landscape' from the school of Gaspard Poussin and another from the school of Claude Lorraine are both typical of these 17th century French schools, the latter being peopled by swains, country wenches and other improbable figures.

Among 18th and 19th century pictures are local scenes, such as 'Wakefield Bridge and Chantry' by Philip Reinagle; good portraits – George Romney's of the Revd Daniel Wilson and Philippe Mercier's earlier rendition of Mrs Shakespeare; and paintings of everyday life, the most famous of which is James Tissot's 'The Thames' (1876), with a boating picnic group against a background of smoky, ship-filled riverscape. There are also interesting 19th century watercolours, including a 'Landscape with Cattle' by Peter de Wint.

The gallery has good paintings by famous and less well-known British 20th century artists. Among the former, Ben Nicholson, Harold Gilman and John Piper are of note. But I rather like 'Needham's Farm' by Harry Epworth Allen, in his distinctive style of stacking up lines in a landscape, 'Misty Morning on the Somme' by George Graham, and 'Pontefract, New Hall' by Fred Lawson, with its strong colours.

More recent than these paintings is the outstanding 'Gwen John in Paris' by Pat Douthwaite, oil and acrylic on linen, featuring prominent black hat, red lips, black cigarette and tuft of armpit hair. I also like 'Self Portrait by the Window' by Oleg Kudryashov, a wild study. 'Two Women' by Bruce McLean and 'Figurative Landscape' in terracotta by Helaine Blumenfield were two of a number of intriguing works on display when I was last there. The gallery has further interesting modern works of art, which make it well worth a visit when you are next in this ancient heart of the West Riding.

WHITBY

Whitby Museum

Pannett Park, Whitby, North Yorkshire YO21 3JW
(0947) 602908
Closed Sunday mornings, and on Monday and Tuesday afternoons October to April.
♿: very little space around showcases to manoeuvre wheelchairs.
 & write to the Hon. Secretary in advance.

Step back in time in this, the favourite museum of many curators. Hardly changed for decades, Whitby Museum contains quantities of wonderful objects from the locality and from different parts of the world, reminders of Whitby's rich past as a seaport.

Two galleries are devoted to the maritime connection. One of these contains relics associated with three famous seafarers – Captain James Cook, and the Scoresbys, Senior and Junior. Cook learned his seamanship in Whitby in the 18th century (there is also a *Captain Cook Memorial Museum* here in Grape Lane); on all of his monumental voyages of discovery he sailed in Whitby-built ships. The museum has manuscripts written by Cook, including the only known surviving part of the original draft of his *Journal*, describing his voyage towards the South Pole in 1773–4. A sea-chest is said to have belonged to Cook.

Pacific Islands material is colourful and varied. A specimen of native cloth from Tahiti was brought to Whitby by Cook himself. Paddles from a chief's canoe from the Tubuai Islands; carved wooden pigs from Trobriand, New Guinea; ceremonial swords with shark's teeth from the Gilbert Islands; throwing clubs and a war club from Fiji; a leg ornament of shells and teeth from Hawaii; shell money, ceremonial adzes and shield: all jostle for space in the museum cases. Objects from Australia and New Zealand include engraved emu eggs, stone axes, adzes and clubs, a 'teko teko' carved figure, a Maori feather cloak and treasure box, model war canoes, and two tattooed Maori heads, which are those of chieftains slain in battle, claimed as trophies.

William Scoresby Senior (1760–1829) and Junior (1789–1857) were both whaling captains, the latter becoming a clergyman and scientist. The museum has narwhal tusks, one almost nine feet long, whale baleen, scrimshaw work, harpoons for whaling and sealing, and a harpoon gun by Wallis of Hull. Scoresby Senior's cabin chair is here, with a dental plate carved from walrus ivory (I'm not sure much improvement has been made in dental-plate design since). There are plants brought back by Scoresby Junior from Greenland in 1822, and the last bird collected by him still in existence, a Greenland Falcon. Scoresby's scientific instruments are housed in the case purchased shortly after his death by the museum, including the Horseshoe Magnet of Nine Bars made in Greenland. Another instrument is a splendid orrery of about 1830, built to demonstrate the motion of the planets and

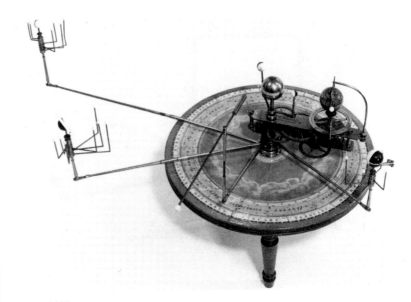

Orrery, c.1830

moons. From the Scoresbys' house comes a cast iron pump of 1819 with the message (in Latin): 'Water for the free use of all / Draw it / Drink it / But don't stand around gossiping'.

The Shipping Wing of the museum contains scores of ship models, the best of which are quite magnificent. The 'Cutty Sark' is here, the fastest sailing ship of them all. The builder's model of the first trawler to fish out of Scarborough can be seen alongside a model of the Viking Gokstad ship, the collier brig 'Lord Nelson', and many more of all types. A superb model of a three-decker French man-of-war, made entirely of ivory (including the rigging), was bought in 1870 by a Captain Rayment from a drunken Frenchman in Dieppe, in exchange for two cases of beer.

The lifeboat models include one of the vessel built by Mr Falkingbridge in 1860. In February 1861 this boat rescued the crews of six ships in a gale, but overturned trying to save a seventh only sixty yards from the pier. Eleven out of the twelve crew were drowned. Harry Freeman, the sole survivor, can be seen in a noble photograph by the great Whitby photographer, Frank Meadow Sutcliffe. Freeman's lifebelt is also on display.

French prisoners-of-war in the Napoleonic wars often built model ships during their captivity, which they could then sell. The models were made

View of ship model displays in the Shipping Wing

out of bones from their rations, sometimes using human hair for rigging, and there are some very fine examples in Whitby. One, a 74-gun ship, is said to be older than usual, dated around 1756–60. Another is made from walrus ivory. A third is a ship-of-the-line of about 1788, with 120 guns.

Quadrants and sextants are displayed in quantity, with telescopes and other naval instruments. A tiny 'New Globe of the Earth' by L. Cushee of about 1790 is in its own shark-skin (shagreen) case. A portable compass-and-sundial in ivory was made by Michael Lesell in Nuremburg in the early 16th century.

Two curiosities are, firstly, the doorpost from the blacksmith's in Church Street, Whitby, used to try out ships' branding irons in the early 19th century, such as 'Sappho', 'Orion', 'Mariner' and 'Whitby'; and, secondly, a piece of bar-shot that penetrated HMS 'Revenge' through a bridle port at the Battle of Trafalgar, killing a midshipman. Equally curious are the large numbers of ships-in-bottles – I still don't know how they do it.

Whitby has fascinating collections of material brought back to the port by seafarers from Africa and Asia. The African items include pottery from Northern Algeria and Zulu ornaments, while a Burmese Goudama Buddha, Japanese ivories and armour, and Indi-

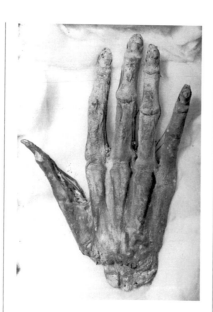

The 'Hand of Glory'

an figures representing different types of villager (snake-charmer, fish-seller, dancing woman, grass-cutter, and more) are of great interest.

Further local collections are tremendously varied. Among the natural history and geology specimens are some mighty beasts. Biggest of these is the *Ichthyosaurus crassimanus*, over twenty-three feet long, accompanied by an 1856 handbill advertising its exhibition. This animal was a swimming reptile of about 150,000,000 years ago. A second large fossil is *Teleosaurus chapmani*, a crocodile found in the local alum shale in 1824. There are lots of examples of more recent animal life, especially seabirds.

The rest of the museum is full of an extraordinary mixture. A reef coral from the Great Barrier Reef is a mass of colour. The ceramics feature Chelsea, Bow and Derby porcelain, with some Rockingham china dogs. The jewellery ranges from Victorian hair jewellery (including that of Adelaide Ann Procter, the poet) to a large amount of pieces made from the local jet (the museum has probably the best collection of Whitby jet in Britain). Snuff boxes, samplers, knitting sheaths, gingerbread moulds,

surgeon's and dentist's equipment, an 18th century clarinet, pipes, matchboxes, dolls, horse brasses, coins, tokens and banknotes, and costume, are all here to be discovered, with a water-bottle from Marston Moor, a 17th century treasure chest, a crossbow of the early 19th century for killing rooks and rabbits, finds from Whitby Abbey such as an Anglo-Saxon runic comb, and Grandad Wormald's first clogs. A bizarre broadsheet advertises Mr. Tomkinson the Clown and his newly invented patent stomach pump, 'allowed to be the most laughable scene ever witnessed by an audience . . .', with graphic illustrations. That's entertainment!

The 'Hand of Glory' is the hand of a murderer severed while the body was on the gibbet, and shaped to be used as a candle holder. This, and talismans like it, were steeped in salt, saltpetre and pepper before being dried, to be used by a burglar with a candle made from the fat of the same corpse mixed with wax. The judicious use of incantations would then enable the burglar to charm house occupants to sleep, and to unbolt doors. Not for the squeamish, though.

The Tempest Prognosticator was invented to forecast the weather by Dr Merryweather (no joke), a former curator of the museum. It involves leeches, pint bottles, whalebones and bells – if you want to know how it works you will have to visit the museum.

Two 17th century portraits of Captain Browne Bushell and his wife, of Bagdale Hall, and an 18th century 'A Quaint Picture of Witby' are among the small number of paintings in the museum, although the adjacent art gallery (to which admission is free) does have more, the best of which are 'Whitby' by Henry Redmore and 'Rotterdam in 1839' by George Chambers.

Add to all of this the archaeological collections, some photographs by F.M. Sutcliffe, firearms, Queen Victoria's nightdress, and the crocodile donations box, and you have a wonderland of history that every museum-lover should seek out. And it is surrounded by the most fabulous countryside.

Detail of French man-of-war model

YORK

National Railway Museum

*Leeman Road, York, North Yorkshire
YO2 4XJ   (0904) 621261*
Open daily. 🚇🚻🅿 ♿W
🚹 & 🚻 contact Education Service
to book and for details of
comprehensive educational
services. ◉
Mother and baby room.
Reference Library.

'No waste or shavings to be used in
these closets. Any person detected in
disobeying this order will be severely
dealt with.
April 8th 1891   By order.'

   . . . and who knows what that might
involve? While the National Railway
Museum is dominated by locomotives,
there is a great deal else to see if one
can be torn away from the gleaming
monsters standing around the two
turntables in the centre of this converted steam-locomotive shed. Notices
about toilets are prominent among the
extensive collections of signs, which
are often all that is left today of railway
stations (or locomotives for that matter).

   The story of the railways is quite
fascinating, as recounted in a series of
displays set aside from the locomotives
themselves. The idea of vehicles moving on rails evolved slowly, the Romans
first using stone tracks for wagons and
carts, as found on Watling Street. In
medieval Europe, miners used wooden
planks as rails for underground
wagons, while British coalmines began
using purpose-made wooden rails, and
later iron ones. All these methods of
transport employed either man or
horsepower. In 1804, at Pen-y-darran
in South Wales, Richard Trevithick set
his steam locomotive to haul loaded
trucks along the iron rails of the local
wagonway – the world's first railway
train. He displayed his engine 'Catch-
me-who-can' in London in 1808,
offering rides at a shilling a time.

   Other landmarks followed, the
Stockton and Darlington Railway
being the world's first public railway to
use steam locomotives; in 1825 the
engine 'Locomotion' was the first to
haul a trainload of passengers. George
Stephenson was responsible for much
progress at this time in locomotive
design. The museum has a large number of small exhibits tracing these and
later developments, such as manuscripts, railway company seals, models
of locomotives, timetables, maps, uniforms, ticket nippers, tickets, oil lamps,
railway watches and inkwells, works
plates – the list is endless.

   The display, 'Toys and Treasures',
includes Wills cigarette cards issued in
1939, and other cards of locomotives
given away with ice-cream in the
1930s. There is a cardboard 'Flying
Scotsman' made during the Depress-
ion, using pencil for axles and old
photographs for the body. *The Comic
Bradshaw*, subtitled 'Bubbles from the
Boiler', is an 1848 spoof of the real
Bradshaw, which was a serious railway
guide. A children's book recites:

'I is the iron from which rails are made,
And J is the Junction where two lines
are laid.
K is the Key, which fastens the door
When the carriage is full, and will not
hold one more.'

   Games, cutouts, postcards, tin models and other curiosities demonstrate
the grip that railways have held on
some people's imaginations.

   Railway companies owned shipping
lines as well as railways, and these are
represented in model ships, and a very
nice model of cabin accommodation on
board the SS 'Duke of Lancaster' in
1928.

   Photographs of NUR pickets, china,
uniforms, and truncheons all form part
of the Story of the Railways, which
contains the museum's most uncon-
vincing exhibit – a London & North
Eastern Railway platform refreshment
trolley of about 1925, nicknamed 'The
Hearse', with plastic (or is it real ?)
food on board.

   Another part of the museum not
dominated by locomotives and rolling
stock is the Front Gallery, which is
devoted to paintings, prints, posters
and photographs. Exhibitions of these
items change quite frequently, but include some of the museum's most

Cabin accommodation on the SS 'Duke of Lancaster'

The 'Agenoria', built in 1829

The Advanced Passenger Train (APT)

memorable images. You can see famous railway posters such as 'Speed', a winged figure originally modelled in clay, produced by Bertram Mackennal for the London, Midland & Scottish Railway in 1924 (ill. on cover). 'East Coast Joys' is a series of posters advertising the LNER painted by Tom Purvis in the late 1920s, the flat colouring of which was to be copied throughout the world of advertising. The museum's varied collection of paintings numbers over a thousand, and includes Victorian narrative pictures and 20th century works, such as 'The Return to the Front' (1928) by Richard Jack.

You can expect to see up to fifty locomotives at the museum. The oldest

is the Shutt End Colliery 0-4-0, 'Agenoria', built in 1829 (the museum has a 1979 replica of the 'Rocket', which was also built in 1829). The newest is the Advanced Passenger Train, designed to tilt when going round bends (remember?). The ancient locomotives include the 1845 Grand Junction Railway 2–2–2 'Columbine', an influential design and the oldest preserved express locomotive, and the 1846 0–4–0 No.3 'Coppernob', which worked until 1900.

The biggest locomotive is the Chinese National Railways 4–8–4 (1935), which is over ninety feet long and weighs 116 tonnes. It was one of a group of twenty-four built in England and sent to work on the steep gradients of the Canton-Hankow and Nanking-Shanghai lines. The London, Midland & Scottish Railway 'Princess Coronation' 4–6–2 'Duchess of Hamilton' (1938), and the British Railways Class 9F 2–10–0 'Evening Star' (1960) are two of the best-known locomotives. The 'Duchess' is of the class that produced the highest sustained power output of any steam locomotive recorded in this county. The 'Evening Star' was the last steam locomotive to be built by British Railways.

Undoubtedly the star locomotive at the museum is the LNER 4–6–2 Class A4 'Mallard' (1938). On 3rd July 1938, 'Mallard' broke the world speed record for steam locomotives, reaching 126 mph descending Stoke Bank, south of Grantham. Its distinctive streamlined shape is a superb example of 1930s design.

Among the rolling stock are some very luxurious carriages, notably Queen Adelaide's Coach (London & Birmingham Railway, 1842) with its gold-plated handles, and Queen Victoria's Saloon (London & North Western Railway, 1869), supposedly Victoria's favourite railway vehicle. Two more saloons were built in 1902 for Edward VII and Queen Alexandra (one each), and on these, too, no expense was spared. The Pullman Parlour Car 'Topaz' (1913) is at once opulent and classy, having been restored to its 1920s style.

More mundane is the LMS Third-

First, Second and Third Class, from the 'Comic Bradshaw'

The 'Mallard'

Interior of Pullman Parlour Car, 'Topaz'

York Castle Museum

York, North Yorkshire YO1 1RY
(0904) 653611
Open daily. 🕐 ▣
& ST: wheelchair access to
ground floor only (includes
reconstructed streets), ▣ (with a
helper).
⑪ & ⑪ should book in advance:
phone (0904) 33932 weekday
afternoons. Extra educational
facilities for ⑪ from North
Yorkshire: contact Education
Officer (0904) 653611. ☺

One of the region's major attractions,
York Castle Museum has immense
collections based on a gift made in
1935 to the City of York by Dr J.L.
Kirk, a country physician with magpie
tendencies of unstoppable proportions.

Much of the Kirk collection is displayed in Kirkgate, the famous reconstructed Victorian Street named after
him, and the visitor with plenty of time
will see hosts of fascinating objects
through the shop windows, and in
Kirkgate itself, Post Office Court, and
Princess Mary Court. There are telescopes, microscopes, precision instruments and a lantern slide projector in
Cooke the Opticians, in Princess Mary
Court. Iddison, Dealer in Cricketing
Material, in Post Office Court, sells
bows and arrows, lacrosse racquets,
golf clubs and cricket bats. Roger Iddison, proprieter, was captain of Yorkshire CCC from 1863–70; his most
famous feat was going on strike in
1865. A photograph in the shop window shows him proudly alongside
George Freeman, the fastest bowler of
his era, who in 1867 took fifty-one
wickets at only 7.4 runs each. Nowadays, Yorkshire fields bowlers who take
seven wickets at 51.4 runs each. Come
back George!

A Highland soldier draws us into the
tobacco and snuff manufacturer and
dealer, the sweet smell of candy tempts
us into the shop of Joseph Terry, con-
fectioner. There is a silversmith, a
grocer, a spirit and wine merchant, a
pewterer, a coppersmith, an apothecary
and druggist, a posting-house and

Class Sleeping Car (1928) with its
foldaway bunks, which is much more
like what most of us are used to. Even
more lowly are the freight and service
vehicles, of which the museum has a
large collection. The earliest is the
Peak Forest Canal Co. Truck of 1797,
the oldest preserved vehicle in Britain
that runs on track, once used in limestone quarries. More evocative is the

Cramlington Colliery chaldron wagon
of 1826, which used to have a bucket
filled with glowing coal to act as a tail
lamp.

There is much else to see – clocks,
nameplates, photographs, winding engines, turntables, even horsedrawn
vehicles. A visit to the National Railway
Museum will make you look at rail
journeys in a different light.

1953 Coronation sitting room

coach office, a toyman and haber-dasher, a tallow chandler, a bank, a musical-instrument maker, a police station (with cell), a fire station (with fire engines), a watchmaker, a bookseller and stationer, and Ebenezer Ellerker, the costumier and pawnbroker. Kirkgate's shop fronts are authentic, and so are the objects inside; but they have been brought together in a pastiche of how we would like to see Victorian life rather than how it really was.

Complementing Victorian Kirkgate is Edwardian Half Moon Court. By now the motor-car was replacing the horse-drawn carriage, and Wales and Son, Carriage Builder and Motor Body Builder, do business at the end of the court. Nearby is a mobile butcher's wagon and (for some reason) a Gypsy caravan. The King William IV Hotel has good beds for cyclists, and a working Polyphon, but sadly sells no beer. Meanwhile, if you need anything, the local ironmonger probably has it.

The most realistic stuffed dog in any museum sits in front of a fire in a reconstructed Moorland Cottage of the

Juke box

1860s, the contents of which show the transition from the traditional way of life to the age of mass-production.

Staffordshire dogs and glass walking-sticks share the room with a witch ball, set in the window to reflect away the stare of a witch.

In addition to a 17th century 'Yeoman's Hall', a Georgian Room, and a Victorian Parlour, there is a 1953 'best' room, with its Murphy television set, flying ducks on the wall, and imitation-leather three-piece suite. More recent is a 1981 kitchen, which is contrasted with a 1940s kitchen; both appear in a gallery devoted to hearths and cooking.

20th century design is conveyed by a Juke Box, a 1930s teapot (registration number OK T42), a 'Sgt Pepper's Lonely Hearts Club Band' record sleeve, and a beautiful 1920s sequinned-dress panel, designed when the Egyptian sytle became popular in the wake of the discovery of the tomb of Tutankhamun. More designs are on view in a gallery devoted to domestic items, such as vacuum cleaners, heaters, lighting, washing machines, televisions and radios.

There is a great miscellany of other wonders: keys, horse brasses, truncheons, fire insurance marks, knitting sheaths, valentine cards, silhouettes, a collection of early agricultural implements, a medieval moorland cross, Staffordshire figures, and a slipware posset pot of Thomas Toft. Among my favourites are Gilligan's Grand Juvenile Galloping Ponies; a spillwork rattle inscribed with charms and mottoes, which probably belonged to a village 'cunning man'; and the portrait of Old Henry Jenkins, Yorkshire's oldest man (or biggest liar), who was said to be 169 years old when he died in 1670 at Bolton-on-Swale. Old Henry claimed to have taken a horse-load of arrows to Northallerton for the Battle of Flodden (1513), and to have been at Fountains Abbey frequently before the Dissolution of the Monasteries in the 1530s. Don't miss Pat the Giant's head, which looks down morosely at visitors, possibly wondering where the rest of his 254 stones of bull disappeared to.

The most famous exhibit in the Castle Museum is probably the Condemned Cell, with its toilet, its cat o' five tails, and its scold's bridles. There are the irons reputedly worn by twelve-

1640s tract from display on the Civil War in Yorkshire

Jolson penny-in-the-slot machine

Gilligans Grand Juvenile Galloping Ponies

year-old Anne Brooks, who was executed in York in 1717 for poisoning her master and mistress, and the pathetic tiny manacles used to restrain children.

The Castle has a magnificent and very extensive collection of weapons and armour. A selection of items is on display in the Military Gallery, which at the time of going to press is being rearranged to concentrate on the Civil War. The museum's Civil War armour is impressive, and includes finds from the field of the Battle of Marston Moor, fought just a few miles outside York.

The star exhibit in the Military Gallery is the Anglo-Saxon York Helmet of 700–750 AD, which was found at the Coppergate site in York. It is in extremely good condition, made of iron with brass fittings, and sporting a chainmail neck protector. It is, with the Benty Grange helmet in **Sheffield City Museum**, and the Sutton Hoo helmet in the British Museum, among the best of all Anglo-Saxon military finds.

The Castle Museum also has notable collections of costume and costume accessories, and a range of dolls and toys. The three-storey Heslington Baby House of 1715, an early example of a dolls' house, is displayed along with clockwork toys, fans, haircombs, and jewellery. A small number of costumes are shown in thematic settings, and are changed frequently. They include good examples from the early 19th century, and from the 1920s. Most unusual when I visited was a fancy dress in the form of a First World War ration book. More unusual still was the shoe of William Bradley, the 'Gigantic Yorkshire Giant' (1787–1820), who was 7′ 9″ tall and weighed twenty-seven stone, and was exhibited in a travelling circus.

All this, and Al Jolson singing 'Toot Toot Tootsie' – a towering performance worth travelling miles to see!

York City Art Gallery

Exhibition Square, York, North Yorkshire YO1 2EW (0904) 623839
Open daily. **F** &
& book in advance.

Visitors to York often miss the Art Gallery, which is a great pity because it houses an art collection of the highest quality. It contains a wide range of post-medieval west-European painting, and there is also an outstanding collection of modern stoneware pottery.

Pride of place must go to the Old Master collection, among which Italian and Dutch paintings stand out. The two earliest Italian works are 'The Dead Christ with the Virgin and St John', and 'The Virgin and Child Enthroned' and 'The Crucifixion' (the latter two wings of a triptych) respectively by the Master of the San Lucchese Altarpiece and by Puccio di Simone (both active mid-14th century in Florence). 'St Peter' and 'St Paul' are by Martino di Bartolommeo (active 1389–1434 in Siena). These works are all devotional, and were painted long before the laws of perspective were applied in art during the Renaissance to suggest three-dimensional depth. The colours are marvellous.

Bernardino Fungai (1460–1516) painted scenes from the life of St Clement, of which York has 'St Clement Striking the Rock' and 'The Martyrdom of St Clement'. St Clement was sent to Roman stone quarries for refusing to abandon his faith, and led by the Lamb of God, relieved the thirst of other condemned Christians and convicts by striking a rock from which sprang water. He was martyred by being tied to an anchor and thrown into the sea. Both paintings are vivid and colourful, but poor old St Clement!

Italian art had changed dramatically by the time Bernardo Licinio (*c.* 1490–*c.* 1550) painted the 'Portrait of a Musician' and Parmigianino (1503–40) painted the 'Portrait of a Man with a Book'. Both are lifelike portraits, the latter of a dark and brooding figure. Parmigianino is a particularly curious

Bernardino Fungai, The Martyrdom of St Clement, *c.1500*

Domenichino, Monsignor Agucchi, *c.1621–1623*

character, whose work was influential on contemporary and later painters. He spent time in prison and, according to the Renaissance biographer Vasari, turned to alchemy, which changed him into a wild man.

A later, 17th century Italian portrait is that of Monsignor Agucchi by Domenichino, a friend of the sitter.

Agucchi, secretary to Pope Gregory XV, was also a writer on art. He is pictured holding a sheet of paper, and wearing a cleric's *biretta* or cap. From the 18th century come two townscapes. One is 'Il Rio dei Mendicanti' by Francesco Guardi, a contemporary of Canaletto. The other is the wonderful 'The Piazza San Martino and the Duomo, Lucca' by Canaletto's nephew, Bernardo Bellotto. Bellotto used a *camera obscura* to help him produce such finely-crafted views, this one with sunshine playing across the square casting long shadows, the buildings painted with great fidelity.

A triptych dating from around 1500 is the earliest Dutch painting, portraying Christ before his judges in the centre panel, with scenes from the Old Testament on the wings, featuring David and Goliath, Samson and Jonah. 'Portrait of a Man', attributed to Jan van Scorel (1495–1562), is a noble portrait by a Dutch master who introduced Italian influences to north European art. Moving to the 17th century, 'Roman Charity: Cimon and Pero' is by Dirck van Baburen, a follower of Caravaggio, and shows a scene from ancient history wherein Pero suckles her father Cimon, a general, con-

Franz Snyders, A Game Stall, *c.1625*

demned to starve in prison. Jan van Goyen was an important and prolific painter, whose 'Peasants and Horsemen at an Inn', with its subdued tones and a typical van Goyen low horizon, rewards close study.

The richness of York's Dutch 17th century paintings is revealed by the wide variety of subject matter and style. 'Bathsheba' is a half-length nude in profile by Paulus Bor. Jan Victors was a pupil of Rembrandt, and painted scenes of everyday life; 'The Butcher's Shop' is a scene outside a butcher's, a pig hanging on a caumerill being dressed. A 'Battle Scene' by Philips Wouwerman, a pupil of Frans Hals, shows an engagement between cavalry and infantry, which emphasises the brutality of such conflict. More gory still is 'Jael and Sisera' by Jan de Bray: after the battle between Sisera's forces and the Israelites, Sisera fled to the tent of Jael, wife of an ally, who is depicted here driving a nail into his head with a hammer.

'Coast Scene with Lobster Catchers' by the versatile Nicolaes Berchem is a romanticised coastal view, while 'Seascape with Galliots' by Abraham Hendricksz van Beyeren shows ships heeling over in a squall. A second painting by

Francis Cotes, The Hon. Lady Stanhope and the Countess of Effingham, *c.1767/70*

Van Beyeren, 'Still Life: Banquet Piece', is a sumptuous picture. 'Vanitas' by Juriaan van Streek is a moral piece stressing the fleeting nature of life, and features a globe, helmet, violin, bugle and other symbolic items. Finally, 'Interior of the Church of St

Bavo, Haarlem' is a softly-lit view of this superb but austere protestant church by Isaac van Nikkelen.

The Flemish 17th century paintings at York are fewer in number than the Dutch works, but among them are 'Portrait of a Lady' by David Teniers the younger, 'Portrait of a Young Girl' by Cornelis de Vos, the lavish 'A Game Stall' by Franz Snyders, an accomplished assistant of Rubens, and 'Still Life with Fish and Cat' by Alexander Adriaenssen.

European Old Masters other than the Italian, Dutch and Flemish include 'Flagellation of St Barbara' from the German workshop of the Younger Master of the Schotten Altarpiece (late 15th century), and 'Sleeping Soldier' by the German Bernhard Strigel (1461–1528). 'Still Life with Citrus Fruits' is by a Spanish painter rarely seen in this country, Luis Egidio Melendez (1716–80). 'Le Défilé', a battle scene, is an equally rare early work by the Frenchman, Antoine Watteau (1684–1721), best known for his languorous scenes of elegantly-dressed figures in park-like settings.

Though not of quite the same quality as the continental paintings, the pre-19th century British paintings at York are nonetheless interesting. In particular they offer a survey of portraiture over more than two centuries, and illustrate especially well the role played by foreign artists working in England. 'Alberte de Ligne, Prince of Barbançon and Arenberg' is by Anthony van Dyck, who altered the course of portraiture in Britain. 'A Scene from the Play, "The Careless Husband"' is by Philip Mercier, portraying a husband, Sir Charles Easy, found compromised with the maid. Other 18th century paintings include 'Lady Stanhope and the Countess of Effingham as Diana and her Companion', the masterpiece of Francis Cotes, and 'Captain John Foote' by Sir Joshua Reynolds. The 'Portrait of Miss Elizabeth Heathcote' is a cute but charming study by York-born Lewis Vaslet (1732–1808). The strangest painting, however, is 'Prospero' by the Romantic painter and hair fetishist, teacher of Constable, Etty and others, the Swiss-born Henry Fuseli.

York has a large number of works by locally-born William Etty (1787–1849). He is most famous for his nudes, as seen in many life studies and a typical piece made especially for exhibition, 'Hero and Leander' (a long-term loan). However, other interesting works include the dramatic 'Bridge of Sighs, Venice', copies after Titian and Rubens, and portraits such as the striking study of Mlle Rachel, the French tragic actress.

19th and 20th century British works at York are very wide-ranging. The nucleus of the Victorian collection is a group of pictures of everyday life, to which a stark contrast is provided by several apocalyptic scenes of roughly the same period. 'Armageddon' by Joseph Paul Pettit outdoes even the spectacular John Martin, whose 'Christ Stilleth the Tempest' is quite calm by comparison! Martin it was whose insane brother tried to burn down York Minster. J.M.W. Turner's 'Rievaulx Abbey' (on loan) is a lovely painting, with the beautiful Abbey swathed in light. 'Landscape', a small early work by Richard Dadd, was painted before the artist murdered his father. Dadd spent most of his life in lunatic asy-lums, and is best known for his fairy pictures.

The gallery is particularly rich in works by followers of James McNeill Whistler and by the early 20th century British artists known as the Camden Town Group. 'Nocturne in Blue and Gold' was probably begun by Whistler but finished by Walter Greaves. 'View from a Canal Bridge, Chalk Farm Road' by Spencer Gore is a good example of the second category. 'Girl in a Red Shawl' by Gwen John and 'Winter Sea' by Paul Nash are fine examples of each artist's work. Two paintings by L.S. Lowry, one of 'Clifford's Tower, York', are typical of the artist's compositions, and there are similarly representative works by Henry Tonks, Tristram Hillier and David Bomberg.

Among a small group of French 19th century paintings are works by Theodore Rousseau, Eugéne-Gabriel Isabey and Henri Fantin-Latour. Best of all for me was a brilliant landscape by Jean Corot, 'Wood Gatherers' (a loan).

York is a gallery much underrated by the public, and its collections well deserved wider notice.

Paul Nash, Winter Sea, *1925–37*

Yorkshire Museum

Museum Gardens, York, North Yorkshire YO1 2DR   (0904) 629745
Open daily. 🚻 ♿ W
🚻 & ♿ book in advance; North Yorkshire schools 🆓, reduced admission rates for others. ◎

The historic city of York, formerly known variously as Eburacum (Roman), Eoforwic (Anglo-Saxon) and Jorvik (Viking) is an unbelievably rich archaeological site. A great many of the finds made underneath this modern tourist Mecca are now displayed in the Yorkshire Museum.

The building itself is a fine example of Georgian Greek revival style, and was purpose-built by the Yorkshire Philosophical Society in 1827–29. It stands in botanical gardens in the centre of the city, which also contain the ruins of St Mary's Abbey, a corner tower of the Roman fortress of Eburacum, and a Georgian Observatory.

Eburacum, Roman York, grew from a small trading centre on the south bank of the river Ouse into the provincial capital of Lower Britain in the 3rd century AD, with a legionary fortress on the north bank. Evidence of the strong military presence is abundant in the museum, in the form of cavalry harness, a fragment of a leather tent, spearheads, ballista balls (thrown from catapults), caltrops (iron prongs strewn on the ground to disable enemy horsemen), and the blade of that most effective of weapons, the all-conquering legionary iron sword. Across the centuries this blade proclaims the might of the Roman Empire.

The tombstone of Lucius Duccius Rufinus, Standard Bearer of the Ninth legion, who died aged twenty-eight, points to the fact that life could be short on the frontiers of the Empire. Lucius's Legion, consisting of some 5,300 men, was the force that broke the resistance of the Brigantes, the principal British tribe in the North, after 71 AD. It was to garrison this Legion that the fortress at York was built. The 'disappearance' of the Ninth Legion after 108 AD gave rise to the legend that it was annihilated by British tribesmen, although it is more likely that it was withdrawn from Britain. The Legion is last recorded in a gate inscription dated 107–8 AD, on display in the museum, and in popular belief remains the Lost Legion.

Two heads in the museum also say much about life in this Roman frontier province. The earlier of the two was severed from its owner's body at the Brigantian stronghold of Stanwick, perhaps to decorate a gate as a war trophy before the site was abandoned towards the end of the 1st century AD. The skull suffered three severe wounds, one of which saw the slicing off of a section at the front, probably from the death-blow. The second head is less gruesome. It is a marble sculpture of Constantine the Great, proclaimed Emperor of Rome by his troops at York in 306 AD. The sculpture, the earliest surviving one of Constantine, is renowned for its portrayal of power

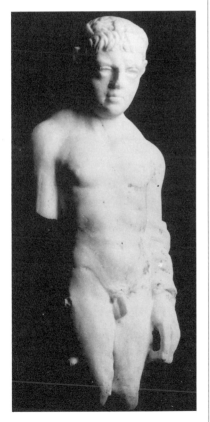

Roman marble statue of an athlete

and virility. Constantine was a brilliant general, whose lasting fame rests on his tolerance of the Christian Church.

Not all Roman life was warlike, and the museum has displays on reading and writing, with board-game counters of bone, glass and stone, and bone dice. There is a mirror of copper-tin alloy, haircombs, hair pins of jet and bronze, jet pendants, the ivory handles of a lady's fan, bracelets and brooches of bronze, dress fasteners, gold rings, a necklace of amber and blue glass beads, even shoes and stockings. A small, exquisite marble statue of an athlete has retained its vigour through the centuries.

A cobbler's last, metalworking tools, the Knaresborough hoard of metal bowls, strainers and dishes (said to have filled a cart when discovered in the 19th century, though much of it was melted down before it was recognised as being Roman), bronze and bone kneedles, spindle whorls, pottery – all are evidence of the craft industries needed to keep the Empire supplied with domestic goods as well as instruments of war. Wall paintings from Roman Catterick (Cataractonium) and the 'Four Seasons' mosaic depicting Summer with a rake, Winter with bare twigs, Autumn with grapes, and Spring with a bird, reveal something of Roman interior decoration.

Like most societies, the Romans were preoccupied with death and religion. Corpses were buried with grave goods, such as bracelets, necklaces and beads, and tombstones were often erected, like the one of Lucius Duccius Rufinus. Another tombstone in the Yorkshire Museum is that set up in York by Gaius Aeresius Saenus, veteran of the Sixth Legion (which replaced the Ninth in York in about 122 AD), to Flavia Augustina, who died aged thirty-nine, her daughter, and her son, Saenius Augustus (aged one year and three days). A large stone sarcophagus is all that is left to us of Julia Fortunata. An extraordinary relic of Roman death is a gypsum cast of a mother and baby, who were covered in gypsum, possibly in an attempt to preserve the bodies, when buried in 4th century Clementhorpe.

Roman pottery mask from Catterick

A stone relief of the god Mithras, slaying a bull to release the power of its blood, was discovered in a Mithraic temple in Micklegate, York. It now resides in the museum near a life-size statue of Mars, the god of War, and tiny figures of Bacchus (god of Nature and Wine), a bronze Mercury (god of Commerce), a bronze Vulcan (the smith-god), and a pipeclay Venus (goddess of Love) rising from the sea. A face-mask of pottery unearthed at Catterick, complete with horns, was probably used in religious performances in a temple or theatre as part of the rituals of another cult. Found with an infant burial in the foundations of a wall are six amulets, with hand, scallop shell (representing the womb) and phallus joined together, all to bring good luck to the building.

Britain was abandoned by the Romans at the beginning of the 5th century AD, and it is believed that York fell to the Anglo-Saxon invaders/settlers in about 600 AD. The Yorkshire Museum has objects from the Anglo-Saxon period from various parts of Yorkshire and Humberside. This was a warlike age, represented by arms and armour, and in particular the splendid 9th century sword from Gilling West, with silver strips applied to its grip, guard and pommel.

St John the Evangelist from St Mary's Abbey

The Ormside Bowl is a particularly lovely 8th century bowl with a silver-gilt outer shell, found buried in the churchyard at Ormside, possibly to save it from plundering Vikings. The museum has a second bowl, of the 7th century, with a base decorated with applied silver foil, this one possibly used for holy water. Other items from the Anglo-Saxon period include two fragments of an ecclesiastical chair of the 8th century from Lastingham, probably the Abbot's throne. Curiously, one of these fragments is on loan to the museum from a church, the other from another museum. The chair-end terminates in a dragon's head, a popular motif in Northumbrian art.

The finest item among the Viking-age collections is a silk cap found at Coppergate in York, matched almost for quality by two silver brooches, and antler and bone skates, combs and pins. Leather items from Pavement in York include a child's boots. More in keeping with the popular image of Vikings are a battle-axe and swords.

Post-Norman Conquest material begins with a hoard of 600 silver pennies from Jubbergate, which were deposited in 1068/9 and were never recovered. These would have been sufficient to purchase 2,000 sheep. A statue of around 1160, possibly from the West Front of St Mary's Abbey, may be the best figure sculpture of its date in England. Other relics of St Mary's include a stained glass medallion of the 14th century, and another glass image of an angel playing a gittern. The best of the Chapter House sculptures is that of St John the Evangelist. A bell-metal mortar from the Infirmary is exceptional.

Almost unexpectedly, the Yorkshire Museum also has an extensive collection of pottery and porcelain. Particularly well represented are Delftware, early slipware, and Rockingham and Leeds pottery. Staffordshire pottery includes one of those bears with a detachable head, a drinking vessel commonly found in museum collections, but this one has a baby bear too. Another good piece is an early 18th century Fuddling Cup, an earthenware ring of tubular clay standing on three feet with six cups mounted on it, and a single mouthpiece to drain the whole lot.

A trip to York is never complete without a visit to the haven of the Yorkshire Museum gardens. Dodge the peacocks and the squirrels, and go and see the latest exhibition.

Yorkshire Museum of Farming

Murtonpark, Murton, York, North Yorkshire YO1 3UF   (0904) 489966 Open March to October. 🆔 ▣ 🅿
🚹: most of museum **W**, Mezzanine **A** (stairs), **G**; many of the museum artefacts and livestock may be touched by the blind.
🚻 & 🚻 contact Education Officer to book and for details of extensive range of activities and facilities; reduced admission rates for 🚻. ◎

Britain's greatest surviving industry is celebrated in a museum that ranges over the story of farming in Yorkshire's broad acres, four million in all – as many as there are letters in the Bible, we are told.

Yorkshire is indeed a vast canvas (well, it was until the bureaucrats dismembered the 1,000-year-old county in 1974), and virtually all types of British agriculture have been found here, from the thinnest of livestock-based hill farming to the record-breaking crop-growing of the Humber warplands and coal measures.

The key to successful farming is drainage, as Roman, Anglo-Saxon and medieval farmers were aware long before Cornelius Vermuyden brought Dutch drainage skills to Yorkshire in the 17th century. Since then, drainage has been based largely on underground clay pipes, and more recently, on plastic pipes. Among the museum's ditching spades, drainage spades and pipes the extraordinary Buckeye Trencher stands as a monument to farming inventiveness (surpassed in design only by the sail reaper – see below!).

Winter ploughing is the next stage in preparing agricultural soils, the plough in many ways being the prime symbol of farming success. Originally dragged by humans, ploughs have since been drawn by cattle, horses, steam engines and tractors. A number of varieties are on view, one drawn by a horse, another by a powerful Caterpillar crawler tractor of 1939, imported from the USA to aid Britain's war effort.

Indeed, the theme of power runs right through the museum, both in a superb collection of photographs, and in the shape of tractors, engines, ox yokes, horse collars, and other items. Of the tractors, the Fordson and the Ferguson TE 20 (the 'Little Grey Fergie') were once familiar sights in Britain's fields. Less familiar was the Ferguson Model A tractor, known as the Ferguson-Brown after its designer, Harry Ferguson, and manufacturer, David Brown of Huddersfield. Only some 1,350 of these were built between the wars, but they incorporated hydraulic lift and three-point linkage, and were extremely light, providing a pattern for all future tractor production.

Spring is the traditional time for preparing a seed-bed through manuring, harrowing and rolling. Seeding was done entirely by hand until the development of the seed fiddle and the seed drill. The drills at Murton range in size up to the tractor-drawn combined seed and manure drill by Russells of Kirbymoorside.

Summer is for lazy picnics, agricultural shows, crop growth and protection, and haymaking. Scarecrows are perhaps more familiar in books than they ever were in the fields. The scythe is another symbol of farming that has had a very long history, though mechanisation has seen it all but disappear from the hayfields. A huge hay elevator (the National Stacker) suggests why the scythe was overwhelmed in the quest for ever-greater production; a cumbersome hay press shows that inventiveness does not always result in good ideas.

Late summer and autumn bring the harvest, the culmination of the farming year. Sickles and scythes ceased long ago to be used to cut corn as mechanisation brought in turn the tip reaper, the sail reaper, the binder, and finally the combine harvester. Of these the sail reaper was a short-lived device, the design of which is remarkable in its improbability. The root harvest is less romantic, but the machines designed to speed up the process are just as weird.

Barns and granaries have always contained a huge variety of machines and handtools. Chaff cutters, stone-grinding mills, weighs, sack barrows, winnowers, barley hummelers, turnip choppers, hay spades, flails, and cake crushers are representative. Other miscellaneous items range from thatching tools to traps, among these

Caterpillar crawler tractor R2, 1939

The Buckeye land drainage machine

Wensleydale Shearling ram

Pulpit and pews in the museum's reconstructed chapel

the vicious Anglo Impassable mole trap and pole traps. On a larger scale are the beautiful Yorkshire wagons, and threshing machines.

Livestock farming is the other mainstay of Yorkshire's agriculture. The movable shepherd's hut introduces sheep farming. Shepherd's crooks, sheep cratches, sheep shears, branding irons, and a sheep and calf ambulance, are complemented by wonderful photographs of Dales sheep husbandry. Lambing, gelding, tailing, marketing, washing, and clipping are explained, while a starring role is played by local breeds such as Wensleydales and Swaledales.

Pigs are highly intelligent animals, factory-farmed for meat in ever-increasing numbers as pork consumption grows. The tools of the butcher are the fitting centrepieces of the pig displays – killing axes, meat hooks, caumerills, scalding tubs, a pig creel, pig scrapers – along with the pigs themselves. A pig and sheep-weigh seems quite harmless in comparison.

Dairy farming is less gruesome, with its milk pails, milk measures, cheese presses, butter churns, milk yokes, milking parlour and bull staffs. The droving of cattle and the famous Yorkshire cattle fairs are other parts of the story.

The vet is a key figure in livestock husbandry, and the tools of the trade are *most* curious: potions and salves, nippers, cutters, slicers, clamps, syringes. The contents of the castrating tool box are quite indescribable,

though blades and crushers are prominent . . . Some of the equipment here was used by the real-life vet who has become better known as James Herriot.

Beyond the confines of the fields, Murton has much else to offer. Ploughing certificates and championship rosettes remind us of shows and competitions. Model reapers by Bamletts of Thirsk show fine craftsmanship on a miniature scale. A dovecot, duckpond, bee garden and paddocks all have livestock of one kind or another, as horses, cattle, sheep, pigs, poultry and goats mingle. A reconstructed Methodist chapel indicates a strong religious strand in farming life. F.R. Stubbs's ironmongery sells all manner of farming tools and equipment. And a John Fowler diesel locomotive dominates the last surviving stretch of the Derwent Valley Light Railway.

Murton manages to blend some of our more romantic notions of country life with the sober realism of land exploitation and livestock husbandry in a way that is all too rare in rural life museums.

Other Museums in North East England

ALNWICK

Alnwick Castle Museum
The Castle, Alnwick, Northumberland
NE66 1NQ   (0665) 602207
Archaeology collections.

Royal Northumberland Fusiliers Regimental Museum
The Abbot's Tower, Alnwick Castle,
Alnwick, Northumberland NE66 1NG
Regimental collections.

ASHINGTON

Woodhorn Church Museum
Woodhorn Village, Ashington,
Northumberland   (0670) 817371
Local, natural and ecclesiastical
history, crafts.

Woodhorn Colliery Museum
Woodhorn Village, Ashington,
Northumberland   (0670) 856968
Mining museum.

AYSGARTH

Yorkshire Museum of Carriages & Horse Drawn Vehicles
Yore Mills, Aysgarth Falls, Aysgarth,
North Yorkshire DL8 3S2
(0748) 3275
Transport museum with coaches and
carriages.

BAILDON

Bracken Hall Countryside Centre
Glen Road, Baildon, Shipley, West
Yorkshire BD17 5EA
(0274) 584140
Local and natural history with garden
classroom, guided walks.

BAMBURGH

Grace Darling Museum
1 Radcliffe Road, Bamburgh,
Northumberland NE69 7BT
Collections relating to sea heroine
Grace Darling.

BARDON MILL

Vindolanda Museum
Chesterholm, Bardon Mill, Hexham,
Northumberland NE47 7JN
(049) 84277
Archaeology museum at site of Roman
fort.

BARNSLEY

Cooper Gallery
Church Street, Barnsley, South
Yorkshire S70 2AH (0226) 242905
17th–19th century European paintings,
English drawings and watercolours.

BARTON-ON-HUMBER

Baysgarth Museum
Baysgarth Park, Caistor Road,
Barton-on-Humber, South
Humberside DN18 6AH
(0652) 32318
18th century mansion in park with
archaeology, geology, local history,
decorative arts.

BATLEY

Batley Art Gallery
Market Place, Batley, West Yorkshire
WF17 5DA   (0924) 473141
Local art in particular.

BEDALE

Bedale Hall Museum
Bedale Hall, Bedale, North Yorkshire
DL8 1AA   (0677) 24604
Country house with local and general
collections.

BEVERLEY

Beverley Art Gallery & Museum
Champney Road, Beverley, North
Humberside HU17 9BQ
(0482) 882255
Local history and art.

BILLINGHAM

Billingham Art Gallery
Town Centre, Billingham,
Cleveland TS23 2LW
(0642) 555443
Modern art.

BRADFORD

Bradford Industrial Museum
Moorside Road, Eccleshill, Bradford,
West Yorkshire BD2 3HP
(0274) 631756
Former spinning mill with textiles,
engineering, transport.

Colour Museum
Perkin House, 82 Gratton Road,
Bradford, West Yorkshire BD1 2JB
(0274) 390955
Museum of colour and light, founded
by Society of Dyers and Colourists.

BRETTON, WEST

Yorkshire Sculpture Park
Bretton Hall, West Bretton,
Wakefield, West Yorkshire WF4 4LG
(0924) 830579
Parkland setting for outdoor sculpture.

BRIDLINGTON

Bayle Gate Museum
Bayle Gate, Bridlington, North
Humberside YO16 5JT
(0262) 71876
Local history and decorative arts in
Augustinan Priory Gatehouse.

Sewerby Hall
Sewerby, Bridlington, North
Humberside YO15 1EA
(0262) 677874
18th century hall in park with archaeology, art, agriculture, and collectons relating to Amy Johnson.

BRIGHOUSE

Smith Art Gallery
Halifax Road, Brighouse, West
Yorkshire HD6 2QJ
(0484) 719222
19th century art gallery in park.

CASTLEFORD

Castleford Museum Room
Castleford Library, Carlton Street,
Castleford, West Yorkshire WF10 1BQ
(0977) 559552
Local history and archaeology, with Castleford pottery.

CAWTHORNE

Cawthorne Victoria Jubilee Museum
Taylor Hill, Cawthorne, South
Yorkshire S75 4HH
Local and natural history, ethnography, in small village museum.

CHESTER-LE-STREET

Ankers House Museum
Church Chare, Chester-le-Street, Co.
Durham DH3 3PZ   (091) 3883295
Medieval anchorage, Roman collections.

CORBRIDGE

Corbridge Roman Site Museum
Corbridge, Northumberland
(043) 4712349
Archaeology museum on Hadrian's Wall.

COXWOLD

Shandy Hall
Coxwold, York, North Yorkshire
YO6 4AD
(03476) 465
Home of Laurence Sterne, author of *Tristram Shandy*, with collections relating to him.

DARLINGTON

Darlington Art Gallery
Crown Streets, Darlington,
Co. Durham
(0325) 462034
19th and 20th century art.

Darlington Museum
Tubwell Row, Darlington, Co.
Durham DL1 1PD
(0325) 463795
Local and natural history.

Darlington Railway Museum
North Road Station,
Station Road, Darlington, Co.
Durham DL3 6ST
(0325) 460532
Restored railway station with locomotives on famous Stockton & Darlington Railway.

DEWSBURY

Dewsbury Exhibition Gallery
Wellington Road, Dewsbury, West
Yorkshire WF14 1HW
(0924) 465151
Local history and art exhibitions.

Dewsbury Museum
Crow Nest Park, Dewsbury, West
Yorkshire WF13 2SA
(0924) 468171
Museum of Childhood in park, with toys and dolls.

DONCASTER

Doncaster Museum & Art Gallery
Chequer Road, Doncaster, South
Yorkshire DN1 2AE   (0302) 734287
Local and natural history, art, King's Own Yorkshire Light Infantry collections.

DURHAM

The Bow Trust
Durham Heritage Centre, St. Mary-
le-Bow, North Bailey, Durham, Co.
Durham DH1 3ET   (091) 3844466
Local history of Durham City.

Durham Light Infantry Museum &
Arts Centre
Aykley Heads, Durham, Co. Durham
DH1 5TU   (091) 3842214
Regimental collections, art exhibitions.

Old Fulling Mill Museum
The Banks, Durham City, Co.
Durham DH1 3EB   (091) 3743623
Archaeology collections.

Ushaw College
Durham, Co. Durham DH7 9RH
(091) 3731254
Medieval religious art.

ELVINGTON

Yorkshire Air Museum
Elvington, York, North Yorkshire
YO4 5AT   (0904) 85595
History of aviation in World War II building, with aircraft.

FORD

Heatherslaw Mill Museum
Ford, Northumberland
(089) 082338
19th century working watermill with milling collections.

FULNECK

Moravian Museum

Fulneck, Fartown, Pudsey, West Yorkshire LS28 8NT (0532) 564069

History of the Moravian Church, lace and embroidery, ethnography.

GOLCAR

Colne Valley Museum

Cliffe Ash, Golcar, West Yorkshire HD7 4PY   (0484) 659762

Local history and textiles in three weavers' cottages.

GOMERSAL

Red House Museum

Oxford Road, Gomersal, Cleckheaton, West Yorkshire BD19 4JP (0274) 872165

17th century house with Brontë connections.

GOOLE

Goole Museum & Art Gallery

Market Square, Carlisle Street, Goole, North Humberside DN14 5AA (0405) 2187

Local history, maritime art.

GRASSINGTON

Upper Wharfedale Museum

The Square, Grassington, Skipton, North Yorkshire BD23 5AQ (0756) 752800

Local history in two 17th century leadminers' cottages.

GREAT AYTON

Captain Cook's Schoolroom Museum

101 High Street, Great Ayton, North Yorkshire TS9 6QH.

Captain Cook and local history in Cook's school.

GRIMSBY

Welholme Galleries

Welholme Road, Great Grimsby, South Humberside DN32 9LP (0472) 242000

Local history, ship models, maritime art.

HALIFAX

Bankfield Museum

Boothtown Road, Halifax, West Yorkshire HX3 6HG (0422) 54823

House in park with toys, costume, regimental collections.

Calderdale Industrial Museum

Central Works, Halifax, West Yorkshire HX1 0QG   (0422) 59031

Industrial history, especially textiles, and period street.

Piece Hall Industrial Museum & Art Gallery

Square Road, Halifax, West Yorkshire HX1 1PR (0422) 59031

18th century Cloth Hall; textiles history, art.

HAREWOOD

Harewood House

Harewood, Leeds, West Yorkshire LS17 9LQ (0532) 886225

18th century house in park, decorative and fine art, furniture, Bird Garden.

HARROGATE

Harrogate Art Gallery

Public Library, Victoria Avenue, Harrogate, North Yorkshire HG1 1EG (0423) 503330

19th and 20th century paintings, watercolours.

Royal Pump Room Museum

Royal Parade, Harrogate, North Yorkshire HG1 2RY (0423) 503340

Local history, pottery, jewellery in former spa building.

HARTLEPOOL

Gray Art Gallery & Museum

Clarence Road, Hartlepool, Cleveland TS24 8BT (0429) 266522

Local and natural history, archaeology, art, period buildings.

Hartlepool Maritime Museum

The Library, Northgate, Hartlepool, Cleveland TS24 OLP (0429) 272814

Maritime history, ship models.

HAWES

Upper Dales Folk Museum

Station Yard, Hawes, North Yorkshire DL8 3NT (09697) 494

Local history of the Dales.

HAWORTH

Brontë Parsonage Museum

Haworth, West Yorkshire BD22 8DR (0535) 42323

Georgian home of the Brontë family, with their furniture and belongings.

HEBDEN BRIDGE

Heptonstall Grammar School Museum

Hebden Bridge, West Yorkshire HX7 7LY (0422) 843788

17th century schoolhouse with local history.

HECKMONDWIKE

Heckmondwike Exhibition Gallery
Walkley Lane, Heckmondwike, West
Yorkshire WF16 ONU
(0924) 403764
Local history and art.

HESSLE

Cliff Mill
Hessle Foreshore, Hessle, North
Humberside HU13 OHB
(0482) 882255
Whiting mill in park next to Humber
Bridge.

HEXHAM

Chesters Roman Fort Museum
Lincoln Inn, Humshaugh,
Hexham, Northumberland
(0434) 81379
Archaeology museum at site of Roman
fort.

Middlemarch Centre for Border
History
The Old Gaol, Hexham,
Northumberland   (0434) 604011
Border history since the 16th century.

HOLMFIRTH

Holmfirth Postcard Museum
Huddersfield Road, Holmfirth, West
Yorkshire HD7 1JH
(0484) 682231
Postcards of the firm Bamforths.

HORNSEA

North Holderness Museum of Village
Life
11 Newbiggin, Hornsea, North
Humberside HU18 1AB
(0964) 533430
Local history of North Holderness.

HORSFORTH

Horsforth Village Museum
The Green, Horsforth,
West Yorkshire LS18 4RH
(0532) 580518
Local history of Horsforth.

HOUSESTEADS

Housesteads Roman Fort Museum
Housesteads,
Northumberland NE47 4NN
(049) 84363
Archaeological museum at site of
Roman fort on Hadrian's Wall.

HUDDERSFIELD

Huddersfield Art Gallery
Princess Alexandra Walk,
Huddersfield,
West Yorkshire HD2 1YF
(0484) 513808
British paintings and sculpture,
especially 20th century.

Tolson Museum
Ravensknowle Park,
Wakefield Road, Huddersfield,
West Yorkshire HD5 8DJ
(0484) 530591
Local and natural history, transport,
archaeology, toys, in museum in park.

HULL

Old Grammar School
South Church Side, Hull, North
Humberside HU1 1RR
(0482) 222737
Elizabethan school and hall with local
history.

Posterngate Gallery
6 Posterngate, Hull, North
Humberside HU1 2JN
(0482) 222745
Contemporary art and photography.

Springhead Museum
Springhead Lane, Hull, North
Humberside HU5 5YJ
Museum of the water industry in
Victorian pumping station.

Spurn Lightship
Hull Marina, Hull, North
Humberside   (0482) 222737
1920s light vessel moored in Hull
Marina.

University of Hull Art Collection
Middleton Hall, Cottingham Road,
Hull, North Humberside HU6 7RX
(0482) 46311
British paintings, drawings, sculpture
1890–1940, and Chinese porcelain.

ILKLEY

Manor House Museum & Art Gallery
Castle Yard, Ilkley, West Yorkshire
LS29 9DT   (0943) 600066
16th and 17th century building with
local history and archaeology.

White Wells
Wells Road, Ilkley,
West Yorkshire LS29 9DT
(0943) 600066
18th century spa bath house with
natural history.

IMMINGHAM

Immingham Museum & Gallery
1/2 Waterworks Street, Immingham,
South Humberside DN40 1AT
Local and natural history, art.

IRESHOPEBURN

Weardale Museum
High House Chapel, Ireshopeburn,
Weardale, Co. Durham
(0388) 537417
Local and natural history, with John
Wesley connection.

KIRKLEATHAM

Kirkleatham Old Hall Museum
Kirkleatham, Redcar, Cleveland
TS10 5NW   (0642) 479500

Queen Anne country house with local
history, gardens.

KNARESBOROUGH

Old Court House Museum
Knaresborough Castle, Castle
Grounds, Knaresborough, North
Yorkshire HG5 8AS   (0423) 503340

Local history in part-medieval building
in castle grounds.

LEEDS

Leeds City Museum
Calverley Street, Leeds, West
Yorkshire LS1 3AA   (0532) 462465

Natural history, archaeology and
ethnography, with aquarium.

Leeds Industrial Museum
Armley Mill, Canal Road, Armley,
Leeds, West Yorkshire LS12 1QF
(0532) 637861

Local industries, textiles, locomotives,
optics, engineering, with grounds.

Museum of the History of Education
Parkinson Court, The University,
Leeds, West Yorkshire LS2 9JT
(0532) 334665

Educational history, schoolwork,
teaching equipment.

Thwaite Mills
Stourton, Leeds, West Yorkshire
LS10 1RP   (0532) 496453

Water-powered crushing mills on
wooded island.

University of Leeds Art Gallery
Parkinson Building, Woodhouse
Lane, Leeds, West Yorkshire LS2 9JT
(0532) 332779

British, European and oriental art.

MALTON

Malton Museum
Town Hall, Market Place, Malton,
North Yorkshire YO17 0LT
(0653) 695136

Archaeology, especially Roman.

MARSDEN

*Tunnel End Canal & Countryside
Centre*
Reddisher Road, Marsden, West
Yorkshire HD7 6NQ
(0484) 846062

Canal museum in tunnel keeper's
cottage.

MICKLEY

Thomas Bewick Birthplace Museum
Cherryburn, Mickley,
Northumberland   (0661) 843276

Engraver's birthplace with print shop.

MIDDLESBROUGH

Cleveland Crafts Centre
57 Gilkes Street, Middlesbrough,
Cleveland TS1 5EL   (0642) 226351

Modern crafts.

Cleveland Gallery
Victoria Road, Middlesbrough,
Cleveland TS1 3QS   (0642) 248155

Fine and decorative art.

Middlesbrough Art Gallery
320 Linthorpe Road,
Middlesbrough, Cleveland TS1 3QY
(0642) 247445

20th century British art.

Newham Grange Leisure Farm
Coulby Newham, Middlesbrough,
Cleveland   (0642) 245432

Farming museum with livestock and
working farm.

MORPETH

Morpeth Chantry Bagpipe Museum
Bridge Street, Morpeth,
Northumberland NE61 1PJ
(0670) 519466

Bagpipes and music in a medieval
chantry.

NEWCASTLE UPON TYNE

The Hatton Gallery
Dept. of Fine Art, The University,
Newcastle upon Tyne,
Tyne & Wear NE1 7RU
(091) 2328511

16th–18th century European paintings,
African sculptures.

John George Joicey Museum
1 City Road, Newcastle upon Tyne,
Tyne & Wear NE1 2AS
(091) 2324562

Local history, period rooms,
regimental collections.

*15th/19th King's Royal Hussars
Regimental Museum*
Fenham Barracks, Newcastle upon
Tyne, Tyne & Wear NE2 4NP
(091) 2329855

Regimental collections.

Trinity Maritime Centre
29 Broad Chare, Newcastle upon
Tyne, Tyne & Wear NE1 3DQ
(091) 2614691

History of the river Tyne.

NORMANBY

Normanby Hall & Country Park
Normanby Hall, nr. Scunthorpe,
South Humberside DN15 9HU
(0724) 720215

Regency mansion in park with
decorative art, furniture, costume.

Normanby Park Farming Museum
Normanby Hall, nr. Scunthorpe,
South Humberside
Farming museum in park.

NORTH SHIELDS

Stephenson Railway Museum Project
Middle Engine Lane, West Chirton
Trading Estate, North Shields, Tyne
& Wear   (091) 2326789
George Stephenson railway material,
with locomotives.

OTLEY

Otley Museum
Civic Centre, Cross Green, Otley,
West Yorkshire LS21 1HD
(0943) 461052
Local history and archaeology.

OVERTON

Yorkshire Mining Museum
Caphouse Colliery, New Road,
Overton, nr. Wakefield, West
Yorkshire WF4 4RF
(0924) 848806
Site museum of mining, with
underground guided tour.

PATELEY BRIDGE

Nidderdale Museum
Council Offices, King Street, Pateley
Bridge, North Yorkshire HG3 5LE
(0423) 711225
Local history of the Dales.

POCKLINGTON

Stewart's Burnby Hall Gardens and
Museum
Burnby Hall, Pocklington, North
Yorkshire YO4 2QE
(0759) 302068
Ethnographic collections with gardens.

PONTEFRACT

Pontefract Museum
Salter Row, Pontefract, West
Yorkshire WF8 1BA (0977) 797289
Local history in art nouveau building.

RICHMOND

Green Howards Museum
Trinity Church Square, Richmond,
North Yorkshire DL10 4QN
(0748) 2133
Regimental collections.

Kiplin Hall
Richmond, North Yorkshire
DL10 6AT   (0748) 818178
17th century house in park, with
furniture, British and European
paintings.

Richmondshire Museum
Ryders Wynd, Richmond, North
Yorkshire DL10 4JA   (0748) 5611
Local history.

RIPON

Ripon Prison and Police Museum
St. Marygate, Ripon, North Yorkshire
HG4 1LX   (0765) 3706
History of law and order in former gaol
and police station.

RIPPONDEN

Ryburn Farm Museum
Ripponden, Sowerby Bridge, West
Yorkshire HX4 4DE
Rural life in small farmhouse and barn.

ROBIN HOOD'S BAY

Robin Hood's Bay & Fylingdales
Museum
Fisherhead, Robin Hood's Bay,
Whitby, North Yorkshire YO22 4ST
Local history; fishing; rural life.

ROTHERHAM

Rotherham Art Gallery
Brian O'Malley Central Library &
Arts Centre, Walker Place,
Rotherham SG5 1JH
(0709) 382121
Paintings; York & Lancaster
Regimental Museum collections.

Rotherham Museum
Clifton Park, Rotherham,
South Yorkshire SG5 2AA
(0709) 382121
18th century house in park with local
and natural history, archaeology,
decorative art, paintings, pottery.

SCARBOROUGH

Crescent Art Gallery
The Crescent, Scarborough, North
Yorkshire YO11 2PW
(0723) 374753
British art.

Rotunda Museum
Museum Terrace,
Vernon Road, Scarborough,
North Yorkshire YO11 2NN
(0723) 374839
Local history and archaeology in
purpose-built early 19th century
building.

Woodend Museum of Natural History
The Crescent, Scarborough, North
Yorkshire YO11 2PW
(0723) 367326
Natural history in former Sitwell
home.

SETTLE

Museum of North Craven Life
6 Chapel Street, Settle, North
Yorkshire BD24 9HS
(0468) 61163
Local history of North Craven; rural
life.

SHEFFIELD

Abbeydale Industrial Hamlet
Abbeydale Road South, Sheffield,
South Yorkshire S7 2QW
(0742) 367731

Restored scythe works; waterwheels;
period houses.

Graves Art Gallery
Surrey Street, Sheffield,
South Yorkshire S1 1X2
(0742) 734781

British and European paintings;
Chinese ivories.

Ruskin Gallery
Norfolk Street, Sheffield,
South Yorkshire S1 2JE
(0742) 734781

Paintings, minerals, manuscripts,
contemporary crafts.

Sheffield Industrial Museum
Kelham Island, Alma Street,
Sheffield, South Yorkshire S3 8RY
(0742) 722106

Iron and steel industry; craft
workshops.

Shepherd Wheel
Whiteley Woods,
Hangingwater Road,
Sheffield, South Yorkshire
(0742) 367731

Cutlery-grinding wheel in park.

South Yorkshire Fire Service Museum
Old Police and Fire Service Building,
West Bar Roundabout, West Bar,
Sheffield, South Yorkshire
(0742) 441881

Fire service history.

SHILDON

Timothy Hackworth Museum
Shildon, Co. Durham
(0388) 816166

Local and railway history.

SHIPTON-BY-BENINGBROUGH

Beningbrough Hall
Shipton-by-Beningbrough, York,
North Yorkshire YO6 1DD
(0904) 470666

Georgian country house in park, with
gardens, and portraits on loan from
National Portrait Gallery, London.

SKIDBY

Skidby Windmill & Museum
Beverley Road, Skidby, Beverley,
North Humberside HU17 5PA
(0482) 862255

Windmill with milling collections.

SKIPTON

Craven Museum
Town Hall, High Street, Skipton,
North Yorkshire BD23 1AH
(0756) 4079

Local and natural history; archaeology
of Craven dales.

SOUTH SHIELDS

Arbeia Roman Fort Museum
Baring Street, South Shields, Tyne &
Wear   (091) 4561369

Archaeology museum at site of Roman
fort.

South Shields Museum & Art Gallery
Ocean Road, South Shields,
Tyne & Wear NE33 2TA
(091) 4568740

Local and natural history; archaeology.

South Shields Volunteer Life Brigade
Watch House, South Pier, South
Shields, Tyne & Wear
(091) 562739

Salvage and equipment associated with
shipwrecks.

STOCKTON-ON-TEES

Green Dragon Yard Heritage Centre
Finkle Street, Stockton on Tees,
Cleveland   (0642) 674308

Local history.

SUNDERLAND

Grindon Close Museum
Grindon Lane, Sunderland,
Tyne & Wear SR4 8HW
(091) 528042

Edwardian Sunderland.

Monkwearmouth Station Museum
North Bridge Street, Sunderland,
Tyne & Wear SR5 1AP
(091) 5677075

Railway history in former Victorian
railway station.

North East Aircraft Museum
Washington Road, Sunderland,
Tyne & Wear

Military aircraft and aero engines.

Ryehope Pumping Station
Ryehope, Sunderland, Tyne & Wear
SR2 0ND   (0783) 210235

Beam-engines in Victorian pumping
station.

THIRSK

Thirsk & District Museum
16 Kirkgate, Thirsk,
North Yorkshire YO7 1PQ
(0845) 22755

Local history.

TYNEMOUTH

Tynemouth Volunteer Life Brigade
Brigate Hut, Tynemouth, Tyne &
Wear

History of the Brigade, with salvage
and equipment associated with
shipwrecks.

WAKEFIELD

Elizabethan Exhibition Gallery
Brook Street, Wakefield, West
Yorkshire WF1 3QW
(0924) 370211
History, art, crafts exhibitions.

Stephen G. Beaumont Museum
Stanley Royd Hospital, Aberford
Road, Wakefield, West Yorkshire
WF1 4DQ   (0924) 375217
Medical history museum.

Wakefield City Museum
Wood Street, Wakefield, West
Yorkshire WF1 2EW
(0924) 370211
Local and natural history; archaeology.

WALLSEND

Wallsend Heritage Centre
Salisbury House, 2 Buddle Street,
Wallsend, Newcastle upon Tyne, Tyne
& Wear   (091) 2620012
Local history, shipbuilding,
archaeology.

WASHINGTON

Washington 'F' Pit Museum
Albany Way, Washington, Tyne &
Wear NE37 1BJ   (091) 4167640
Mining museum.

WHITBY

Captain Cook Memorial Museum
Grape Lane, Whitby, North Yorkshire
YO22 4BE   (0947) 601900
Captain Cook collections in building
where he was apprenticed.

Whitby Archives
17/18 Grape Lane, Whitby, North
Yorkshire YO22 4BE
(0947) 600170
Local history.

WORSBOROUGH

Worsborough Mill Museum
Worsborough, Barnsley,
South Yorkshire S70 5LJ
(0226) 203961
Working 17th century water-powered
corn mill in park.

YORK

Bar Convent Museum
Blossom Street, York, North Yorkshire
YO2 2AH   (0904) 643238
History of Christianity.

Fairfax House
Castlegate, York, North Yorkshire
YO1 1RN (0904) 655543
18th century house with furniture and
decorative art.

Jorvik Viking Centre
Coppergate, York, North Yorkshire
YO1 1NT   (0904) 643211
Viking-period collections and building
remains.

Merchant Adventurers Hall
Fossgate, York, North Yorkshire
YO1 2XD   (0904) 654818
Medieval merchants' hall with
furniture.

York Military Museum
Tower Street, York, North Yorkshire
YO1 1SB   (0904) 642038
Regimental collections.

York Minster Undercroft & Treasury
York Minster, York, North Yorkshire
YO1 2JN (0904) 654134
Church collections, Roman and
Norman foundations.

Index of Subjects

Index of Museum Names

Printed in the United Kingdom for Her
Majesty's Stationery Office
Dd 240079 7/89 C70

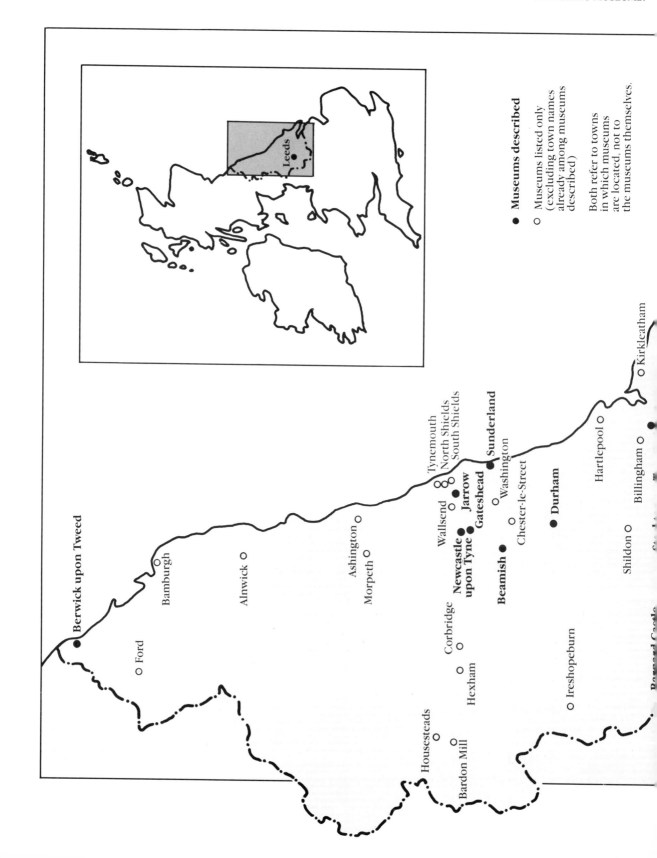

● **Museums described**

○ Museums listed only (excluding town names already among museums described)

Both refer to towns in which museums are located, not to the museums themselves.

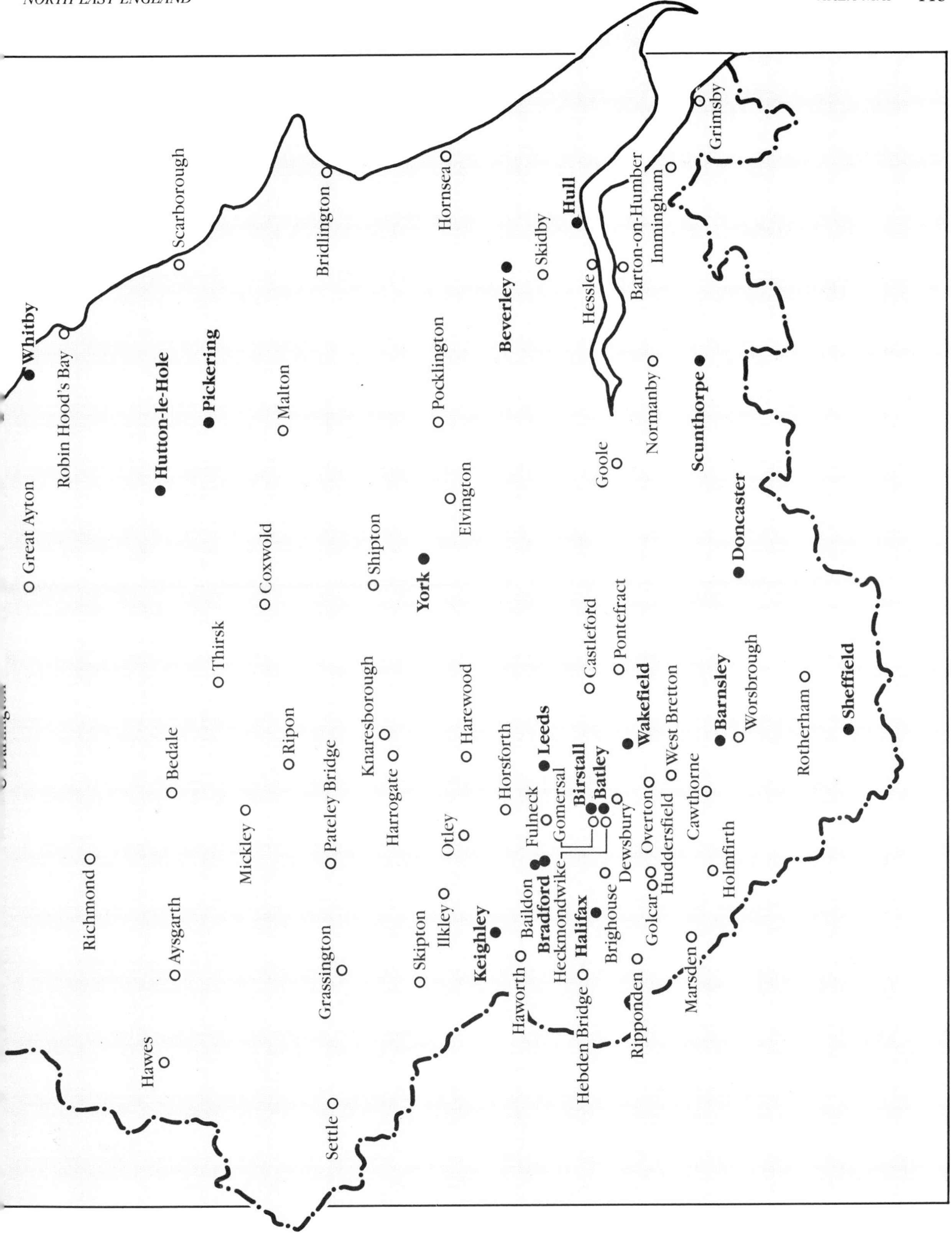

Whitby

Robin Hood's Bay

Great Ayton

Scarborough

Hutton-le-Hole

Pickering

Malton

Coxwold

Shipton

Thirsk

York

Bridlington

Hornsea

Pocklington

Elvington

Beverley

Skidby

Hull

Hessle

Barton-on-Humber

Immingham

Grimsby

Normanby

Goole

Scunthorpe

Doncaster

Knaresborough

Harewood

Castleford

Pontefract

Wakefield

West Bretton

Barnsley

Worsbrough

Sheffield

Rotherham

Leeds

Birstall

Batley

Gomersal

Overton

Cawthorne

Ripon

Pateley Bridge

Mickley

Bedale

Richmond

Aysgarth

Grassington

Skipton

Ilkley

Otley

Horsforth

Fulneck

Baildon

Bradford

Heckmondwike

Dewsbury

Huddersfield

Golcar

Holmfirth

Marsden

Keighley

Haworth

Halifax

Brighouse

Hebden Bridge

Ripponden

Hawes

Settle

Elvington

Pocklington

Bedale